Who the Hell is Jean-Paul Sartre?

Who the Hell is Jean-Paul Sartre?

And what are his theories all about?

Benjamin Jones

First published in Great Britain in 2022 by
Bowden & Brazil Ltd
Felixstowe, Suffolk, UK.

British Library Cataloguing-in-Publication Data
A CIP record for this book is available from The British Library.

Series editor & academic advisor: Dr. Jonathan C.P. Birch, University of Glasgow.

ISBN 978-1-915177-17-9

To find out more about other books and authors in this series,
visit www.whothehellis.co.uk

Contents

Introduction

Asking Jean-Paul Sartre 'Who the hell are you?' taps into the very core of his philosophical concerns, so one should not expect a simple answer. He was a novelist, playwright and journalist – but most of all, he was a philosopher. He wrote two gargantuan texts – *Being and Nothingness* (1943) and *Critique of Dialectical Reason* (1960), as well as countless articles and short works. Alongside his life partner, Simone de Beauvoir (1908–86), Sartre was one half of the power couple that brought existentialism out of academic discourse and into the living rooms of the post-war middle classes. As an intellectual partnership, they utilized the growing radio and TV media to spread the word of existentialism – a philosophy that advocated individual responsibility, spoke out against authority in all its forms, and captured the hearts and minds of disenfranchised youth. For over a decade, Sartre was one of the most important figures in 20th-century philosophy. Even after existentialism had lost momentum, he was still seen as a touchstone for anyone who wanted a razor-sharp analysis of current events that pulled no punches.

Existentialism is a theory that includes the claim that individuals cannot be defined. Similarly, existentialism itself eludes a simplistic definition. If one turns to Sartre's work to find clearly defined terms, there is little to be found. His major works contain glossaries that are less like dictionary definitions than they are repeated attempts to summarize an interconnected set of ideas. Sartre's writing gestures towards concepts, spiralling around them so that each sweep reveals something new, which can leave new readers frustrated and confused. However, if we build a picture of Sartre's ideas in the way we take in the elements of a painting – moving between the parts and the whole so that their relations are changed with every shift – then we can find an enriching and exciting philosophy. This book aims to guide you through some of those complexities, introducing the reader to Sartre's fascinating concepts in an accessible and jargon-free way.

Sartre's philosophy captured the mood of a generation and rallied them against another, so we will begin by looking at his life and the times in which he lived. There will then be a selective overview of some of his key influences before exploring two key concepts within his existentialism: phenomenological ontology and radical freedom. Sadly, the scope of this book does not allow an in-depth analysis of his fiction, nor an engagement with his terrifyingly big *Critique of Dialectical Reason*. However, as this book is as much about who Sartre was as it is about what he thought, we can gain a better insight into the man himself from his views on the role of the intellectual and writer through his understanding of responsibility, which we will look at in the final chapter. From there we can start to reflect upon how Sartre's life and ideas can inform our own.

1. Sartre's Life Story

> *'As a man, if a certain Jean-Paul Sartre is remembered, I would like people to remember the milieu or historical situation in which I lived, [...] how I lived in it, in terms of all the aspirations which I tried to gather up within myself.'* (Sartre quoted in Charlesworth, 1976)

Separating the man from the myth surrounding any figure in history is always a difficult task. With Jean-Paul Sartre, this is exacerbated by his genius at creating his own public image and the tall tales, both celebratory and condemnatory, that were spread around him. Perhaps the best means of approaching Sartre's life is to take everything with a pinch of salt, but to consider how and why he attempted to guide the way the world saw him. Some of this is philosophical, but some of it is deeply personal. A man who lacked confidence in his appearance, but not in his intellect; a leader that spoke out against injustice but was pained by his own silence when it really counted; a child that realized too much too soon, and never fully recovered. If Friedrich Nietzsche (1844–1900) was right in saying that philosophy is the confession of the author – an unconscious revelation of their desires and anxieties – then maybe understanding who Sartre is will help us to understand what he believed.

The Childhood of a Leader

Jean-Paul Charles Aymard Sartre was born in Paris on 21 June 1905 to naval officer Jean-Baptiste Sartre and Anne-Marie (née Schweitzer). The couple had met in Cherbourg in 1903 when Jean-Baptiste was home on leave, and by 1904 they were married. The son of a doctor in the Southwest of France, Jean-Baptiste was a small, slim, sombre young man at just five feet two inches tall (1m 58), with a hugely disproportionate moustache. He had been a brilliant pupil at school, receiving the top award three times in the *concours général* (competitive exams) and his son, Jean-Paul, would grow to be very much like him, both in looks and temperament. Anne-Marie, nicknamed 'You' by her family, was from a prominent, liberal Alsatian family. She stood a head taller than her husband and, by all accounts, was pretty, slim and well-educated, learning to play the piano to an accomplished level (playing Beethoven's most difficult sonatas), sewing, drawing and generally submitting to the role of a young lady of good breeding.

The time of Jean-Paul Sartre's birth saw a lot of political upheaval. The First Russian Revolution had begun, the Russo-Japanese war was in full force, and France was going through its own upheaval with the passing of the law of separation between Church and state which provoked demonstrations and riots. But the birth of Jean-Paul overshadowed all this, and his parents were rapturous with their new arrival. Jean-Baptiste wrote to his parents:

> *'My little Paul is lovely [...] He seems to enjoy everything, he is forever moving, forever excited, he*

> *screams at the top of his lungs, roars with laughter, never cries. [...] I know nothing about children, but I find him very beautiful.'* (Cohen-Solal, 1991)

Sadly, Sartre never knew his father, who died in September 1906. Jean-Baptiste had contracted enterocolitis while stationed in China in 1903 and never fully recovered. Developing bronchitis, his health continued to deteriorate and he was moved back to his childhood home, a small farm near Thiviers, so that his family could help Anne-Marie care for him. Jean-Paul was only 15 months old when Jean-Baptiste finally died aged just 32, leaving Anne-Marie a widow at only 24 years old.

Sartre referred to this as 'the great event of my life' (Sartre, 1967) yet, when speaking of his father, he was dismissive, saying 'We trod the same earth for a while, that is all' (Cohen-Solal, 1991). While it forced Anne-Marie to move back in with her parents in Meudon near Paris, Sartre claimed that it released him from having to be a carbon copy of his father. There were no paternal expectations or instructions to weigh upon him, he said. He was truly free. He had inherited his father's physical appearance, all except for the blond curly hair that he had taken from his mother. Beyond that, he was a blank canvas.

Sartre never had to battle for maternal attention, and he had no other male competition. The pair became a team, with Sartre's unchallenged love for his mother only being reinforced continuously. Oedipal jealousy only emerged later when his mother remarried. For now, he was the most beloved member of the household, named *Poulou* by his mother, and adored by his grandparents. His grandfather, Charles Schweitzer (also

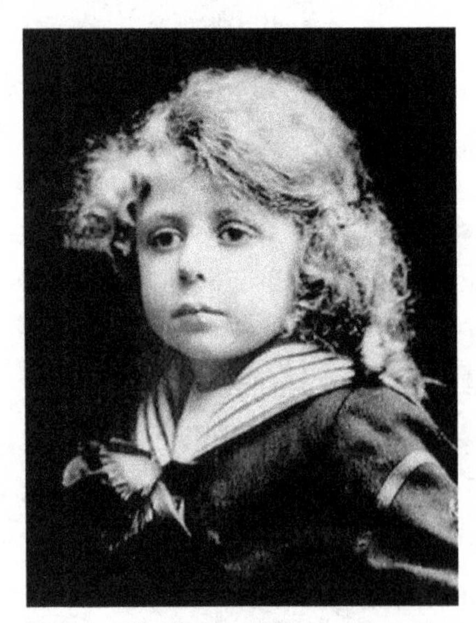

Fig. 1 Jean-Paul Sartre, c.1910

known as Karl), cousin of the Nobel prize-winning polymath Albert Schweitzer (1875–1965), was a teacher in Meudon in the southwestern suburbs of Paris. On the verge of retirement, he continued working to help support Anne-Marie and Jean-Paul, finally retiring in 1911 when he moved the family to Paris. It is through Charles that Sartre made the discoveries that would go on to shape the childhood that his autobiography, *Les Mots* (*Words*, 1964), tells us created the man. Although a teacher, Charles was not a fan of conventional education. He resisted sending Sartre to school until 1913 when eventually Jean-Paul went to the Lycée Montaigne, followed by a public school in Arachon on the southwest coast. He then spent a semester at the Poupon Academy in Paris in 1914. However, none of these schools satisfied Schweitzer's demand to take his child prodigy of a grandson seriously and Jean-Paul's education outside of school took the form of reading Schweitzer's extensive library of classics. 'I began my life as I shall no doubt end it: among books' (Sartre, 1967). In her own act of rebellion against her father, Anne-Marie had treated Jean-Paul to comics and adventure stories, as well as visits to the cinema, both loathed by the classically educated Charles but obsessively consumed by Jean-Paul. 'Even today, I would rather read "thrillers" than Wittgenstein,' Sartre remarked in his autobiography (1967)).

Jean-Paul was a beautiful child with a talent for entertaining guests and delighting his family. A series of incidents slowly undermined this, however, throughout his childhood. Charles had become concerned with the feminizing of his grandson – still carrying his flowing locks at the age of five (or seven depending upon which account you read) – and so, when Anne-Marie was out, he cut the boy's hair. From then on, Jean-Paul noticed the way in which the adults were less willing to entertain him, less forthcoming with their praise. To make matters worse, on a trip to the coast in 1909, he caught a severe cold and contracted leucoma, an eye disease which left him with strabism (crossed-eyes). As a result, he lost 90 percent of the vision in his right eye. Although this would become one of the most recognizable physical features of the adult Sartre, it left him with a realization that never left him: he was ugly.

His childhood became a catalogue of existential crises. At a family gathering, his grandfather had realized that his close friend Emile Simonnot was not present. Scanning the room, Schweitzer announces, 'Someone's lacking here: it's Simonnot' (Sartre, 1967). These words struck the young Sartre. Simonnot was not just absent, as in 'not present'; he was *lacking*. Charles noticed Simonnot's absence. Would anyone miss Jean-Paul when he was missing? Sartre felt utterly superfluous – in his terms, *contingent*. 'I wanted to be missed, like water, bread, or air, by everyone else in every other place' (Sartre, 1967).

From the age of five, Jean-Paul had become obsessed with death, haunted by it at every turn. His only escape was to immortalize himself. At the age of 12 he discovered that he was an atheist, casually realizing this fact while stood at a bus stop waiting for friends. The family home was not deeply religious, although Catholics, Protestants and humanists were all present in his upbringing. 'Deep down it all bored me to death; I was led to unbelief not through conflicting dogma but through my grandparents' indifference' (Sartre, 1967). Sartre realized that one had to create immortality through action. In his case, it would be writing.

In 1917, Anne-Marie remarried. Joseph Mancy, a naval engineer, moved his wife and stepson to the port town of La Rochelle on the west coast of France. Jean-Paul's loathing of Mancy – not only an intrusion into his family life, but also a symbol of the bourgeois life that Sartre was slowly rebelling against – made him channel his resentment into writing. School life in La Rochelle was tough. The boys there were kids from a rough port town. Resentment dwelled in them as most had lost their fathers in WWI, and violence was a standard way of dealing with childhood disagreements. Jean-Paul had to learn how to cope with the bullying, mainly concerning his Parisian accent and unconventional appearance. He retreated into solitude (which meant more writing) but also violence and misbehaviour. After stealing money from his mother, it was decided that Sartre would return to Paris and the Lycée Henri IV. Here he befriended Paul Nizan (1905–40) – a boy who would become a writer and philosopher in his own right – and formed a bond so strong that the pair became known as 'Sarzan and Nitre'. The inseparable duo ended up at the Lycée Louis-Le-Grand in preparation for entry into the famous École Normale Supérieure (ENS). They spent their time together endlessly discussing the literature of the day, speaking as if the characters were real, and sharing their writing with each other. They even developed their own philosophical theories. Perhaps the earliest example of Sartrean thinking appears in their 'theory of the witness', a commitment to simply observe and report on the 'vain agitation of the world' through writing (Hayman, 1986).

L'École Normale Supérieure

Sartre and Nizan entered ENS in 1924. A year earlier, in 1923, *La Revue Sans Titre*, a short-lived magazine subtitled 'journal for the defence of youth', had published Sartre's short story, 'L'Ange du Morbide' ('The Angel of Death') along with several chapters of a novel, *Jesus La Chouette*, both laden with the angst and morbidity associated with Sartre's fiction. This seemed like the literary direction his work would take until he discovered the work of the French philosopher Henri Bergson (1859–1941). Bergson's

Fig. 2 École Normale Supérieure, Paris, c.1900.

understanding of temporality – our internal sense of time as a part of consciousness, rather than the divisible time of science – would reappear in Sartre's own writing in future years. Repeated drafts of the novel *Melancholia* – eventually retitled *La Nausée* (Nausea) - would become increasingly focused on stripping away the raw experiences of the main character, revealing a world of superfluity and nothingness (see Chapter 3).

Sartre was a notorious figure around ENS, not only for his intellect but for his desire to attack the establishment he had grown up around. At one stage, he and his friends sent out a fake press release announcing that ENS was giving an honorary degree to world-famous aviator Charles Lindbergh (1902–74). When the national press and thousands of spectators arrived to find a Lindbergh lookalike, the shame and outrage led the principal of the school to resign. Retribution came when Sartre failed his *agrégation*, his teaching examination (albeit for including too much original thought).

In 1929, Sartre asked René Maheu (1905–75), the third figure in the 'gang of three' with himself and Nizan, to introduce him to a fellow student named Simone de Beauvoir. Maheu had dubbed Beauvoir *Castor*, French for 'beaver', due to her industriousness – a name which stuck. Gradually Sartre and Beauvoir came to know each other through studying together with Nizan and Maheu in Sartre's room. Sartre, typically the most knowledgeable, would sit on the bed or floor, smoking a pipe and explaining the texts patiently to the rest of the enraptured gang of students.

Many saw Sartre as the brooding and isolated philosopher that charmed women by being distant and cool, but such accounts are

Fig. 3 Simone de Beauvoir, date unknown.

far from the truth. He liked to play the clown and was known for his wisecracks and practical jokes. He would perform sketches for Beauvoir, playing out little scenes for her amusement. He would draw pictures, sing songs like 'Old Man River' in his broad baritone, and even make up his own bawdy songs with filthy, scandalous lyrics. Beauvoir's diaries reveal that her main love interest at the time was Maheu, who she referred to as 'Lama'. But over time she grew closer to Sartre. 'Lama makes a woman feel attached to him just by softly caressing her neck, Sartre, by showing her heart to her – which one more surely enslaves her?' (Beauvoir, 2006). On 22 July 1929, Beauvoir wrote:

> *'[For] the 13 days I have known this boy, he has explored me and now anticipates and knows me thoroughly. Intellectual need for his presence, and emotional turmoil in facing his affection [...] I would like him to force me to be a real somebody, and I am*

> *afraid [...] I will give myself over to this man with absolute confidence...'* (Beauvoir, 2006)

His feelings for her were just as powerful: 'There is one thing that hasn't changed and cannot change: that is no matter what happens and what I become, I will become it with you' (Sartre quoted in Rowley, 2007). These words, once written in a letter to Beauvoir, would be placed upon a plaque outside the Hôtel Mistral, Paris, where the pair had resided during the war.

Teacher and Rebel

Sartre took up his national service for 18 months from late 1929. Upon his return, he and Simone lived a relatively decadent student lifestyle, thanks to 80,000 francs left to him in 1930 upon his grandmother's death. Both found work at provincial schools, Sartre in the town of La Havre and Beauvoir in various far-flung reaches across the country. In his solitude, Sartre worked on *Nausea*, redrafting to perfection.

As melancholic as his outlook was, Sartre took great joy from teaching. He earned a reputation among staff and students as an anarchist for allowing his students to smoke in class, attending their beach parties, and wearing a black shirt or polo neck rather than a shirt and tie. He admitted that he felt no fondness for other members of staff and felt closer to his students, who were aged around 18. 'I think it was because I recognised more of myself in them than in older people or those of my own age' (Sartre quoted in Beauvoir, 1985). His teaching methods were founded upon simple principles: 'respect of the students, and the systematic demolition of all the artificial barriers of hierarchy and authority' (Cohen-Solal, 1991). Sartre would enter the room and speak 'off the top of his head, without notes, sitting on his desk' (Giustiniani in Cohen-Solal, 1991). Students would give oral reports which were then openly discussed by the class with everyone treated as equals. There were no sanctions or grades given by Sartre, nor any competition encouraged between pupils. He would sit in bars with his students, sharing cigarettes and singing incredibly vulgar songs that he had concocted himself. This controversial but hugely successful teaching method would eventually lead him to a position in the Lycée Concordet, one of Paris' most prestigious schools.

Meanwhile, Beauvoir and Sartre had to work out how to continue their long-distance relationship. Their love, Sartre said, was necessary. However, there were other relationships that could be *contingent*. His rejection of bourgeois values, coupled with the validation he felt from being sexually desired, led him to suggest that the couple should be willing to see other people. Beauvoir agreed to the arrangement, which was presented as a relationship of pure equality, but the raw facts of the matter were not so simple.

The first signs of this began in 1931 with Olga Kosakiewicz (1915–1983), one of Beauvoir's students. Beauvoir had begun to court Olga and, occasionally, they were lovers. Sartre also became fascinated with Olga and the pair became a trio, with Sartre charming her with the same silly sketches and intellectualism that had captured Beauvoir's heart. Olga brought Sartre back to life following his dark depressive phase and, as much as it pained her, Beauvoir stepped back, allowing Sartre to take her place as Olga's lover. He would write to Beauvoir and tell her intimate details of his time with Olga, as he did with the other women in

Fig. 4 Simone de Beauvoir and Jean-Paul Sartre in Beijing, China, 1955.

his life. Despite this, it seems that Sartre and Olga never fully consummated their relationship. She told him that she didn't love him and that she found him physically repulsive. When the affair ended, Sartre was devastated, professing, 'for the first time in my life, I found myself humble and disarmed before someone' (Rowley, 2007). He continued to support Olga financially, however, and they remained friends: a pattern which continued with his other contingent relationships.

A full exploration of all of Sartre's affairs would take up another volume, but a conversation between Beauvoir and Sartre, captured in her book *Adieux: A Farewell to Sartre* (1981) allowed Beauvoir to publicly interrogate his attitudes towards women, sexuality and her own relationship with him. She claims that as soon as they met he declared that '[he] had no intention of confining [himself] to a single woman'. She puts it to Sartre that, 'It's as though the moment a woman happened to be within your reach, you were perfectly ready to have an affair with her' (Beauvoir, 1981). Sartre describes his attitude to relationships as 'egalitarian', in the way he helps to shape women and allows them to evolve. He also describes his attitude towards women as 'very protective and therefore imperialist' (Beauvoir, 1981).

Sartre would support each woman financially and several, like Olga and her sister Wanda, would be given parts in his plays. He arranged his schedule so that each woman could have time with him as often as possible. His circle of lovers and ex-lovers grew so large that the collective became known as 'The Family'. Sartre kept these contingent relationships 'in a particular world', away from the 'real world' in which he lived with Beauvoir. However, at the core of his world, Sartre admitted that 'The essential was that I should come first. But the idea of a triangle in which there was me and another better-established man – that was a situation I couldn't bear' (Beauvoir, 1981). He may have seen himself as a liberator of women, but his behaviour was patronising at best, and controlling at its worst. His own insecurities stopped him from being the individual that was required for such a complex network of relationships to work without causing harm.

Phenomenologist and Novelist

In 1933, political philosopher Raymond Aron (1905–83), who would go on to become one of France's most prominent thinkers of the 20th century, met Beauvoir and Sartre in the bar Bec de Gaz on Rue Montparnasse in Paris. Aron had discovered the phenomenology of Edmund Husserl (1859–1938), a thinker who attempted to explain the very structure of consciousness through an analysis of first-person experience. Enthusing about the new philosophy he had discovered, Aron told Sartre and Beauvoir that one could talk about a drink and make it into a whole philosophy. Sartre was so taken with these ideas that within a year he was at the French Institute in Berlin, throwing himself into the study of Husserl's phenomenology (which we will explore in Chapter 2) and churning out page-after-page of his own philosophy. This work would become *L'Imagination* (*The Imagination*, 1936), *La Transcendance de l'ego* (*The Transcendence of the Ego*, 1938) and *Esquisse d'une théorie des émotions* (*Outline for a Theory of the Emotions*, 1939), as well as adding a new dimension to (yet another) draft of *Nausea.*

Back in La Havre, Sartre gave himself a punishing regime of reading and writing, alongside frequent travels to see Simone. He would walk the grey, drab streets and recreate them in his ongoing drafts of *Nausea.* He called his fictional city Bouville (literally 'Mud-town') as he drew inspiration from his own isolation. It was at this time that Sartre began his habit of using amphetamine pills from eight o'clock in the morning to keep him awake and sleeping pills to put himself to sleep, although this was not his only drug use. An old friend and psychiatric intern, Daniel Lagache (1903–72), aware of his investigation into the role of the image in consciousness, offered to inject Sartre with the hallucinatory drug mescalin under medical supervision. The experience – involving time and space distortion, and hallucinations of devil fish – badly shook Sartre and remained with him for weeks, to the point where he believed he was lapsing into permanent psychosis. His hallucinations would return when he was at his lowest, appearing as a giant lobster that remained always out of view.

Sartre, now in his 30s, continued to teach. He worked briefly at a school where his refusal to attend meetings led to a fist fight with another member of staff, before moving on to a school in Neuilly, Paris. By this time, he had finally published *Nausea* (1938) to great acclaim (despite numerous rejections), along with a collection of short stories under the title *Le Mur* (*The Wall*, 1939). His growing recognition was beginning to open doors for further publication. He settled in his spiritual home of Paris and was gaining increasing amounts of female attention. The optimism that accompanied this period, however, would be relatively short-lived.

The Radical Conversion

France between the wars may seem scarily familiar to those in the UK in the early 2020s: a country that is economically battered; centrist politics caught between the rise of increasingly vocal far-left and far-right; a global pandemic that killed millions worldwide; anti-immigrant sentiment and distrust of neighbouring nations; concern over the influence of the USA and Russia; and people looking for direction.

Over one million French men had been killed in military service during WWI, with roughly the same number left injured. Sartre had lived alongside the children of these men during his time at La Rochelle. Hundreds of thousands had died of the Spanish Flu, and the 1920s appeared to be one long economic depression. Immigrant labour – plentiful, thanks to the French colonies – was helping to fill the gap but France relied upon German reparations to keep them going. Germany was reluctant to pay, and a constant struggle of negotiation, renegotiation and open economic sabotage raged between the two nations.

The usual gap between left and right within politics was more like a gulf. On one side, a series of right-wing parties grew in strength – notably the nationalist French Social Party and the anti-Semitic French Popular Party. Both exploited the

Fig. 5 Paul Nizan, 1924.

anger France felt at their betrayal by other countries in their appeasement and capitulation to German demands following the Treaty of Versailles (1919). On the other side, the Cartel des Gauches emerged as a left-wing alternative. It opposed France's imperialism and the influence of the Catholic Church within the supposedly secular country. In the wake of WWI, when empires had crumbled, France was reassessing its own relationship with its colonial history. Many middle-class liberals and leftists were uncomfortable, not only with this, but also with the fact that the Catholic Church was so involved. Its attempts to 'civilize' nations that were (in their view) uncivilized had led to violence and segregation. At home, workers were treated poorly and life remained difficult. Rather than blaming others, the left-wing had turned its gaze inwards and sought radical reform inspired by their outward gazing at Soviet Russia after the Revolution. When riots by a coalition of far-right groups swept Paris on 6 February 1934, it was taken as a fascist coup d'état and support for the left-wing Popular Front (FP) increased. A Socialist premier, Léon Blum (1872–1950), was elected and he promised radical social and political reform to support the workers and give them greater freedom.

These reforms were unsuccessful and there was little return on the promises made. By this time, war was returning to Europe. Stalin was in power in the USSR, Hitler was slowly dominating Europe, and France was split between unstable opposing coalitions of left and right. Hitler's forces captured the city of Paris on 14 June 1940, and when France finally surrendered on 25 June, many were happy to know that they were under Nazi rule. Others felt humiliated by Germany and betrayed by their own people, all with the world as their audience.

During this period, Sartre had been openly socialist but oscillated between indifference towards politics in general, and open hostility towards party politics: 'The way I spent my life from a political point of view up until '39 is very vague,' he admitted (Beauvoir, 1985). Nizan was a committed member of the PCF (*Parti Communiste Français*), which Sartre saw as problematic. It was not the commitment to communism that was the issue, but the way in which an individual resigns their freedom to the demands of The Party (whoever they may be).

With the outbreak of WWII, Sartre was called up for military service. However, during this first year he was trapped in what was referred to as the 'Phoney War' of 1939–1940. His national service had trained him in meteorology but, as the French army prepared for action, Sartre spent his days taking the occasional reading from a weather balloon, eating in cafés, playing chess and writing. His days were interrupted by seemingly pointless tasks as part of an authoritarian structure he despised, with people he felt no connection to, and all as part of a war that was not happening.

> *'All at once I found myself part of a mass of men in which I had been given an exact and stupid part to play, a part I was playing opposite other men, dressed as I was in military clothes, whose part was to thwart what we were doing and finally to attack.'* (Beauvoir, 1985)

His letters to Beauvoir were littered with his annoyance at the other men around him. He found any sort of emotional bond with the other men uncomfortable: 'I was becoming what I don't want to be, the master with his disciples, and I didn't like being confided in' (Solal-Cohen, 1991). Sartre the bawdy joker and raconteur disappeared into writing, committing himself to writing a new novel which would later publish as *L'âge de raison* (*The Age of Reason*, 1945). He would perform his daily tasks so that he could disappear into the background unnoticed, then return to his notebooks. He was rude and aggressive to the other privates and took to wearing a sign around his neck, on one side reading 'you may bug me', on the other, stating 'you may not bug me'. But everything changed on Sartre's 35th birthday. He was captured by German forces and sent to Stalag XIII–D (a prisoner-of-war camp) in Trier, near Luxembourg.

> *'I learned what historical truth really was [...] There was a kind of unity among men who were there – an idea of defeat, and idea of being a prisoner, which seemed at that particular time much more important than anything else. All I had learned and written during the years before seemed to me no longer valid nor even as having any content.'* (Sartre in Beauvoir, 1985)

The transformation was immediate. The proximity he now had with the men around him was forced upon them, but unlike his time as a meteorologist, they were unified by their oppression. The camp guards, who were the living embodiments of the stereotypes he had heard about, would slap, kick, and verbally abuse him. Prisoners slept in cramped conditions and used toilets with no privacy. Rather than breaking Sartre, his situation created 'a form of collective life I had not experienced since the École Normale – in other words I was happy' (Solal-Cohen, 1991). The lack of privacy forced conversation between the men and made every action collective rather than individual. Sartre described how they 'lived in a crowd, perpetually touching each other' (Beauvoir, 1985). He slept on the floor with 14 other men, so cramped that even when reading or writing, he would have to be lying down.

The letters he smuggled out of the camp reveal that the old Sartre persisted in many ways. He had already noticed the hierarchy of the camps, with the guards at the top and the well-fed, lice-free nurses in the middle. In one letter, he boasts of his five-week-old beard, as if hygiene were a capitulation to their authority: 'The beard is a mark of personal obstinacy, for we have barbers here, and anyone can get spruced up like a dandy' (Sartre in Beauvoir, 1990). But his fickle side emerged six days later. After being recognized by 'a cute little intellectual who has not a thing in his head except book titles' (Sartre in Beauvoir, 1990) he quickly cleaned himself up. Even if this inmate was a pseudo-intellectual, he was young and attractive, which meant he was competition. 'I'd been repulsively dirty, by choice and semi-mysticism […] Now I'm washing every day' (Sartre, 1994). Nonetheless, a conversion had taken place. 'I had discovered a social world, as it were [...] I had been reshaped, one might say, by the prison camp.' (Sartre in Beauvoir, 1981)

He secured a job as a translator in the infirmary, then as one of the camp's 'artists'. He was paid to write, direct and act in plays for the guards and prisoners, and his 'nativity' – *Bariona or the Thunder's Son* – was performed on Christmas Eve, 1940. The play dealt with Roman imperialism, man's freedom and need for commitment, and the rejection of subservience. No longer was his writing merely about subjective individual experience, but about a form of ethical honesty – an *authenticity* – that had to be lived.

As well as using his free time to work on *The Age of Reason*, he also began a new masterwork. He had been tutoring a fellow prisoner, Marius Perrin, on Heidegger's phenomenology and – all without access to his books – had started to develop what became *L'Être et le néant* (*Being and Nothingness*, 1943). In return, Perrin helped forge a document that certified Sartre as blind so that he could be released from the camp, although an additional account of Sartre's escape involves an elaborate plot whereby he procured official headed notepaper and forged a note permitting a local farmer to collect two prisoners for work in his fields. Sartre, disguised as the farmer, handed over the note and left the camp. However he escaped, his time in the camp had changed him forever. In his conversations with Beauvoir in *Adieux*, he speaks of writing in a café for the first time after leaving the camp. He was astonished by how far apart everyone was in the café. There was so much 'wasted space' (Beauvoir, 1985). He was now a man that thought of collectives as much as individuals and had to philosophize in a way that spoke of the tug-of-war between everyday life and broader history. The individual could no longer be understood in isolation.

As with his comments about the café, Sartre's reflections on his time in the camps would be spoken about with a sense of nostalgia, not just because of the enlightenment he gained from his time there, but also because he was happy.

From Direct Action to Intellectual Action

> *'He had not come back to Paris to enjoy the sweets of freedom, he told me, but to act. How? [...] We had to unite, to organise a resistance movement.'* (Beauvoir, 1962)

When Sartre returned to Paris, both he and his home had changed. He went back to teaching, this time at Lycée Pasteur in Neuilly, but was less rebellious and unwilling to discuss his time in the camp (his students were even made to take dictated notes). He was more politically aware, more socially conscious, and more dedicated to forcing political change. Sartre explained to Beauvoir that, since leaving the camp, he felt a 'vague feeling of regret for the collective life from which I had been forever severed' and had realized that his apolitical stance prior to the war was something he was ashamed of. The camps had taught him 'a kind of socialism – a dismal kind' that did not take the form of any recognizable socialism of that day and age, but embodied ideas of equality and freedom that, he told Beauvoir, 'was my political tendency then and I've never changed it' (Beauvoir, 1985).

In 1941, he set up the short-lived Resistance group *Socialisme et Liberté* with, among others, the phenomenologist and Marxist Maurice Merleau-Ponty (1908–61) and, of course, Beauvoir. According to another member of the group, ethnologist Jean Pouillon (1916–2002),

> '*. . . we were not an organized Resistance group, we were just a bunch of friends who had decided to be anti-Nazis together, and to communicate our convictions to others. Besides, at a moment when Resistance movements were really beginning to get structured, a group like ours, isolated and with no exterior contact, couldn't possibly stand the test.*' (Pouillon quoted in Cohen-Solal, 1991)

Sartre's most admirable traits – his enthusiasm, intellect, charm and industriousness – propelled the group from a handful of intellectuals into a collective of 50 by 1941. However, as Merleau-Ponty explained: 'Born of enthusiasm [. . .] our little group contracted a fever and died a year later, of not knowing what to do' (Cohen-Solal, 1991). There were many reasons for this failure. Sartre thought and acted as if he were the first to suggest the idea of resistance, yet had no idea of how to organize a national grassroots movement. One member, Jean-Toussaint Desanti (1914–2002), describes Sartre as being unaware, and even unconcerned, of the difficulties of transforming his ethical and ideological arguments 'into real political practice, whose modalities had to be controlled day

Fig. 6 Maurice Merleau-Ponty, date unknown.

by day' (Cohen-Solal, 1991). Some of their activities teetered between naïve and farcical. Members would walk the streets openly carrying a copying machine underneath their arm. A briefcase containing the identities of all members was lost and then recovered at the Lost and Found Office on rue des Morillons. Sartre produced a 100-page constitution for post-war France, thinking that this would be the document to propel the resistance forward, only to have the woman in charge of smuggling it flush the sole copy of the document down a toilet in a moment of nervousness. There was a constant balancing act between the dedicated Marxists within the group and those who were not, so Marxists and non-Marxists would take it in turns to lead the collective. In the end, in a whimper rather than a bang, the group collapsed. They were no match for the principal Resistance groups who were primarily either Gaullists or Communists. Sartre would have nothing to do with either side, unlike his fellow members who, one by one, joined the ranks of the communist PCF.

Following the collapse of the Resistance group, Sartre began submitting work to underground papers like *Combat* and *Les Lettres Français*. He wrote an overtly political play called *Les Mouches* (*The Flies*, 1943) – a retelling of the ancient Greek play *Electra* (c.410 BCE) by Euripides (c.480–406 BCE). Despite its disappointing reception, it made Sartre realize where he could be most useful and his focus shifted. Together with Beauvoir, Merleau-Ponty and old ENS comrade Raymond Aron, he set up the journal *Les Temps Modernes* (*Modern Times*, LTM) in 1944. Having recognized his lack of ability to organize direct action, he decided that he would use his skills as a writer and thinker for his ideological struggles. He would create the intellectual edifice upon which the future could be built.

The Existentialist

Sartre finally published his first masterpiece *L'être et le néant* (*Being and Nothingness*) in 1943, while he was still trying to find his feet as a playwright, journalist and resistance fighter. It was after the war ended that Sartre began his most prolific period of writing – between 1946 and 1949 he produced over 40 works. French writer Jacques Audiberti (1899–1965) described Sartre as having 'five brains'; like 'a truck parking everywhere with great commotion, in the library, in the theatre, at the movies' (Cohen-Solal, 1991). His social life consisted of literary events and theatrical soirées. He was rubbing shoulders with Picasso (1881–1973), Dora Marr (1907–97), Miró (1893–1983), Georges Bataille (1897–1962) and other surrealists in Parisian cafés; although his income was meagre, and his lodgings were less than hygienic. He spent two months in America as a journalist for *Combat* and *Le Figaro* – his first flight and first time outside of Europe –where he met President Franklin D. Roosevelt (1882–1945). He even wrote the song, 'La Rue des Blancs-Manteaux' for the actress and singer Juliette Gréco (1927–2020). Alongside producing numerous plays and articles, he gave a public lecture – published as *Existentialism is a Humanism* (1946) – where the room was so full that people fainted. He produced an existentialist account of anti-Semitism, *Réflexions sur la question juive* (1946, published in English as *Anti-semite and Jew* in 1948); a biography of Baudelaire (1946); essays on writing in *What is Literature?* (1947); and an aborted project on ethics. *The*

Age of Reason became the first book in a trilogy called *Les chemins de la liberté* (*Roads to Freedom*) including *Le sursis* (*The Reprieve*, 1945) and *La mort dans l'âme* (*Death in the Soul*, translated as *Iron in the Soul*, 1949). Written largely in response to the events of WWII and the Nazi occupation in France, the trilogy reflects Sartre's conception of ultimate freedom. The principal character, philosophy teacher Matthieu, undergoes a moment of conversion and commits himself to resistance and the freedom of all. Over the next two decades he would continue to write works that attempted to reflect the brutality of the real world and promote an off-kilter optimism about the possibility of human redemption. His plays touched upon existentialist themes such as The Other in (*Huis clos* (*No Exit/In Camera*) 1944), bad faith and authenticity (*Les mains salles* (*Dirty Hands*, 1948)), as well as political issues like segregation (*La putain respectueuse* (*The Respectful Prostitute*, 1946).

The philosophy that emerged from this era was dubbed 'existentialism' by the philosopher Gabriel Marcel (1889–1973) in 1943. The name stuck and infamy was secured when the Catholic Church placed Sartre's writing – past, present and future – on their list of prohibited books in 1948. With the existentialist writer Albert Camus (1913–1960)

Fig. 7 Albert Camus, 1945.

releasing his second novel, *La peste* (*The Plague*) in 1947, and Beauvoir releasing *Le deuxième sexe* (*The Second Sex*) in 1949, the movement was underway. Sartre was able to finally quit teaching and concentrate on writing.

Difficult Relationships

As time went on, Sartre became estranged from many people who had once been important to him. Raymond Aron fell out with Sartre in 1947 over what he saw as Sartre's dogmatic and quasi-religious attitude towards communism, leading to him quitting LTM. His friendship with Albert Camus would go the same way. Camus and Sartre became friends after Sartre wrote a glowing review of Camus' first novel, *L'Etranger* (*The Stranger*, 1942). The two men struck up a brotherly camaraderie, with shared conversations about philosophy and women. But Camus perhaps brought out the best and the worst in Sartre. From the start, he viewed Camus as the inferior thinker. His review of Camus' novel was arrogantly entitled 'An Explanation of *L'Etranger*', as if Camus was not clear of the themes within his own work. One drunken evening, Sartre goaded Camus by prodding him and declaring 'I'm more intelligent than you, huh? More intelligent!' (Todd, 1998). While Sartre had confidence in his status and intellect, he lacked it elsewhere and clearly felt threatened by his friend. Not only did Camus look more like a Hollywood leading man than a philosophical novelist but he was more active in the resistance during WWII than Sartre had been. He was raised in poverty in Algeria, not the privileged bourgeois world that Sartre had lived in. In short, Camus had the credentials that Sartre felt he lacked.

Camus' relationship with Sartre started to break down when Sartre sided with Merleau-Ponty as Camus criticized him for excusing the Moscow show trials (1936–38). Merleau-Ponty had already written an article for LTM (co-signed by Sartre) accepting the discovery of Soviet labour camps, but arguing that this was an unpleasant means to a justifiable end. Camus took this up in *L'Homme révolté* (*The Rebel*, 1952), for which there was no review in LTM for several months. The book was eventually reviewed by LTM's Francis Jeanson (1922–2009), who brutally attacked both the book and author. Camus was given right to reply, but foolishly aimed his response at Sartre, who in turn gave his own rejoinder. The vicious takedown of Camus – including scepticism over his philosophical credentials – meant that they did not speak again. Camus was killed in a car accident in 1960 at the age of just 46. Having never reconciled their friendship, Sartre wrote a heartfelt tribute to his friend which was published in *The Reporter Magazine* on 4 February 1960. He writes:

> *'He and I had quarrelled. A quarrel doesn't matter—even if those who quarrel never see each other again—just another way of living together without losing sight of one another in the narrow little world that is allotted us. It didn't keep me from thinking of him, from feeling that his eyes were on the book or newspaper I was reading and wondering: "What does he think of it? What does he think of it at this moment?"'* (Sartre, 1960)

These events foreshadowed his split with Merleau-Ponty, who also saw an 'ultra-Bolshevism' in Sartre's work. Sartre had spoken out against the USSR and its crimes (notably the suppression of the Hungarian uprising in 1956), but he was still too willing to advocate violence. Merleau-Ponty's increasing hostility towards the USSR was being edited out of issues of LTM, and in 1953 he resigned. From then on, a few difficult encounters occurred between the two – sometimes in person, sometimes in print – until Merleau-Ponty died suddenly from a heart attack in 1961. Once again, Sartre wrote a poignant essay in tribute to his estranged friend, ending with the words:

> *'There is nothing to be concluded from this except that this long friendship, neither done nor undone, obliterated when it was about to be reborn, or broken, remains inside me, an ever-open wound.'* (Sartre quoted in Solal, 1991)

The Committed Writer

By the end of the 1950s, Sartre had begun work on the next phase of his writing. He wished to rescue Marxism, existentialism and psychoanalysis from their own trappings and create an account of history and the individual that respected the role of both within society and politics. He committed himself to developing two volumes entitled *Critique de raison dialectique* (*Critique of Dialectical Reason*), a political masterpiece which would occupy his every waking hour. Alongside this, he worked on a mammoth biography of the author Gustave Flaubert (1821–80) which he called *L'Idiot de la famille* (*The Family Idiot*, 1971), Sartre's third biographical work following on from studies of Charles Baudelaire (1821–67) and Jean Genet (1910–86). Sartre was consuming the amphetamine corydrane, which he chewed like sweets, as well as a bottle a day of the stimulant orthodrine. This prescription drug habit was sending him deaf and left him with no skin left on his tongue from the obsessive tongue movements caused by the amphetamines. The result from this period of intense writing – *Critique of Dialectical Reason* – was published in 1960 and is a staggeringly impressive work, albeit repetitive and badly edited. The second volume was abandoned and work on the *The Family Idiot* took over.

As the decade progressed, Sartre connected the Marxist struggle with anti-colonialism in Africa. In 1955, he came out in support of Algerian rebels who were trying to regain independence from the French. He dedicated page-after-page of his own work and that of LTM in support, as well as writing the play *Les séquestrés d'Altona* (*The Condemned of Altona*, 1960) as a parallel between Nazi occupation and the ongoing war in Algeria. Sartre signed a manifesto of 121 intellectuals calling for civil disobedience. As violence erupted in the streets of Paris, its signatories faced everything from boycotts to arrest, although calls to arrest Sartre were dismissed by President Charles de Gaulles (1890–1970) who responded with 'One does not arrest Voltaire' (Rowley, 2007). Shockingly, assassination attempts were made on Sartre's life. The organisation *l'Armée Secrète* had begun a campaign of violence against Muslims and those who supported Algerian liberation. In 1961, plastic explosives were detonated in the hallway of the apartment building on rue Bonaparte, where Sartre lived with his widowed mother. In 1962, another device exploded, destroying Sartre's apartment and several rooms above. Many philosophers would take such a moment to review their position on political violence, but not Sartre.

It was not just political opponents that had their sights set on Sartre and Beauvoir at this point. Ideological allies (or at least those that thought they were) would invite the pair all over the world to build support for their political causes. In 1960, Sartre and Beauvoir were invited to Cuba to meet Fidel Castro (1926–2016) and Ernesto 'Che' Guevara (1928–1967). Sartre found them both to be friendly and keen for their visitor to present the best view of Cuba that they could. He also visited Brazil for three months as an unofficial spokesman for Castroism. President de Gaulle's government had spoken out against the rise of socialism in South America and having a French intellectual of Sartre's calibre speaking out in support of their movement would have been a great boost. Nikita Khrushchev (1894–1971) also sent out an invite which was originally rejected but finally accepted in 1963. Existentialist Marxism's golden couple were the must-have supporters for anyone trying to be seen as a legitimate political presence to the European left. From Sartre's side, this was not just his chance to revel in adulation (or not just that), it was part of his wider commitment to the political struggle, something that he started to wish he had dedicated himself to more in his youth.

A brief dalliance with the mainstream arose during the early 1960s, when Sartre worked on a screenplay about Sigmund Freud (1856–1939) with the director John Huston (1906–1987). However, the project was fraught with conflict and ended with Sartre having his name removed from the credits of the film. This period hints at a more Hollywood Sartre, but this could not be further from the truth. Refusing the Nobel Prize for Literature in 1964 kept the controversy surrounding him alive, as did adopting Arlette Elkaïm (1935–2016) as his daughter so that she could be his literary executrix. She had written to Sartre aged 19 to ask for help with her dissertation. She became his lover for two or three months, but Sartre brought it to an end as his feelings for her were more paternal than romantic. The adoption was not only scandalous to the public, but also to all the other women in his life.

In 1966, Sartre was asked by the 92-year-old philosopher, mathematician and founder of the Campaign for Nuclear Disarmament, Bertrand Russell (1872–1970), to work on his 'International Tribunal against War Crimes in Vietnam'. Sartre was elected executive president and wrote a powerful argument outlining how the tactics used by the United States were not just analogous to genocide – they *were* genocidal. 'All [the USA has] ever done is put this option to the Vietnamese, North and South: either you cease your aggression or we break you' (Sartre, 1974). As much as he was attacking US imperialism, he knew he was doing it through the bourgeois liberal institution of international law. Despite being torn over whether this method conceded too much, the speech published as 'Vietnam: Imperialism and Genocide' in *Between Marxism and Existentialism* (1974) is one of his most stirring reads.

Sartre still had the rebellious credentials. De Gaulle's presidency had created a bored, ignored and increasingly frustrated army of youths. In May 1968, worker and student protests broke out into riots in the streets of Paris. For a moment, the revolution seemed possible. Sartre was one of the many names being held up as either the ideological instigator or philosophical idol of the rioters. Sartre publicly pledged support, telling the world that the violence was a retaliation against the police and the state, not an act of terror. He was still someone the world wanted to listen to.

The Final Years

Spurred on by the on-going violence in France and his work with Russell, Sartre wanted to bring justice directly to those in power and wanted to unite the left in a single struggle, allowing his name to be used to draw attention to a cause. He joined numerous papers, including the revolutionary communist paper *La Cause du Peuple* (*The People's Cause*), as well as setting up his own paper, *J'Accuse* (*I Accuse*). But Sartre still felt he wasn't going in the right direction. The papers only targeted social class and not the plights of minority groups such as homosexuals, women and the young. In July 1973, planning for a new daily paper, *Libération*, began, and is still in publication today. Occupations of the Sacre Coeur, press conferences, feature-length documentaries, a conference on Israel and Palestine held in philosopher Michel Foucault's (1926–84) house – the work never stopped.

Now in his seventies, Sartre's health was failing. He had suffered from high blood pressure for over a decade, and his vast consumption of alcohol, cigarettes and prescription drugs had taken its toll on his body. His eyesight deteriorated quickly due to asphyxiation of the brain caused by smoking (a habit which he continued for several years after doctors warned him of the damage he was doing to his body) and he was left unable to read or write. He would regularly lose his balance and fall and his memory faded.

His work did continue however, thanks to *La Cause du Peuple* editor Benny Lèvy (1945–2003), who became Sartre's personal secretary. He not only read to Sartre but also conducted interviews with him so that four new texts could be co-written, moving towards ethics rather than politics. Lèvy was an expert on Sartre's work, often remembering entire strands of thought that Sartre had forgotten. He was also a fierce intellectual and a political militant, frequently arriving at Sartre's house in a false beard and dark glasses. The 1970s became the decade of Sartre and Lèvy.

Beauvoir, however, feared that Sartre was being manipulated. She was concerned that Lèvy would smuggle his own ideas into publication by using Sartre's name. As a result, her relationship with Lèvy was always frosty and they barely spoke whenever they came into contact. In 1977, Sartre announced in an interview with the far-left political organization Lotta Continua's publication of the same name, that he was no longer a Marxist, which sounded alarm bells for those at LTM and in his friendship group. Too many of the texts Sartre was putting out with Lèvy were anti-Sartrean. In 1978, the pair had recorded a conversation about the Arab-Israeli conflict, followed by a four-day trip to Israel for Sartre to meet intellectuals from both sides to gain enough understanding to write an article for the paper *Nouvel Observateur* (*New Observer*). The resulting work, penned by Lèvy, was badly written and based upon superficial discussions, and the *Nouvel Observateur* refused to publish it. The text was passed on to Beauvoir by one of the journalists at the paper, Jacques-Laurent Bost, Sartre's former student and close friend. The committee of LTM – Beauvoir included – voiced their concerns over the Sartre–Lèvy relationship in a meeting. An explosive argument erupted, and Beauvoir and Lèvy were never in the same room together again. In a typical act of defiance, Sartre distanced himself from his former friends, including Beauvoir.

The confrontation did not end there. Lèvy recorded hours of interviews with Sartre to form the basis of *Power and Freedom*, a text that was intended to be a complete summary of Sartre's political and moral thought. When Beauvoir read the finished text, she cried and threw the manuscript across the room at Sartre. From this point on, two months before his death, Sartre barely saw Beauvoir and divided his time between Lèvy and Arlette. *Power and Freedom* was never published but one final text made it to publication – *Hope Now* (1980) – but perhaps this was not for the best. Published as a conversation with Lèvy, this was Sartre's first substantial work since *The Family Idiot* in 1971. Yet Sartre's answers contain 'flat rhetoric, sluggish thought, [and] weak arguments' (Cohen-Solal, 1991). The sharp thinker with an even sharper wit was gone. It was easy for Lévy's detractors to use this as further ammunition against him, but this could only be bittersweet for Sartre's estranged friends.

On 20 March 1980, Sartre was taken to Broussais hospital in Paris with a pulmonary oedema. On the 13 April, he was visited by Beauvoir. He held her wrist and said 'I love you very much my dear Castor' (Seymour-Jones, 2008). The next day he was unable to speak, except for a few mumbled words. He slipped into a coma and passed away the following day. The crowd that followed Sartre's funeral procession swelled to 50,000 people as it moved from the 14th arrondissement to Montparnasse cemetery. There was no ceremony. Beauvoir sat by his grave on a chair, photographed by the press for the ten minutes or so that she sat in silence. In 1986 Simone de Beauvoir died and was buried next to Sartre in the same grave. Two independent free beings who chose to be together forever as one another's 'necessary love', while others were always contingent.

Jean-Paul Sartre's Timeline

Jean-Paul Sartre

- **1905** Born Jean-Paul Charles Aymard Sartre on 21 June
- **1906** Death of Father
- **1915** Enters Lycée Henri-IV in Paris and befriends Paul Nizan
- **1924** Enters Ecole Normale Supérieure with Nizan and Raymond Aron
- **1929** Meets Simone de Beauvoir
- **1931** Teaches philosophy in La Havre; Starts writing on contingency
- **1933** Discovers phenomenology; Moves to Berlin to study
- **1935** Experiments with mescalin
- **1936** Publishes ***The Imagination and Transcendence of the Ego***
- **1938** Publishes ***Nausea***
- **1939** Publishes ***The Wall*** and ***Outline for a Theory of the Emotions***; Called up for military service
- **1940** Publishes ***The Imaginary***; Becomes prisoner of war
- **1941** Liberated from camp; Forms resistance group with Maurice Merleau-Ponty
- **1943** ***The Flies*** premiers; Publishes ***Being and Nothingness***; Meets Albert Camus
- **1944** ***No Exit*** premiers; First two volumes of ***Roads to Freedom*** and first edition of ***Les Temps Modernes*** published.
- **1945-49** Prolific period of writing and performances, including ***Anti-Semite and Jew***, ***What is Literature?***, ***Dirty Hands*** and the final volume of ***Roads to Freedom***.
- **1947** Split from Aron

World Events

- **1914** Start of World War I
- **1917** Bolshevik revolution in Russia
- **1918** End of World War I
- **1921-24** French disputes with Germany over reparation payments lead to occupation of Ruhr
- **1928** Union of left-wing parties win French elections
- **1934** Right-wing rioting across Paris; General strike across France
- **1936** Popular Front wins elections
- **1939** France and Britain declare war against Germany
- **1940** Germany enters Paris
- **1945** VE Day
- **1947** Revolt against France in Madagascar

1948 Founds short lived RDR; Catholic Church places Sartre on List of Prohibited Books

1950-51 Public condemnation of Soviet concentration camps with Merleau-Ponty

1952 Break with Camus; Meets Heidegger

1953 Break with Merleau-Ponty

1956 Meets Arlette Elkaïm

1957 Publishes ***A Search for a Method***

1959 Works on script for Freud movie and premiers ***Condemned of Altona***

1960 Publishes first volume of ***Critique of Dialectical Reason***

1961 First assassination attempt made

1962 Second attempt on Sartre's life

1964 Publishes ***Words***; Awarded (and refuses) Nobel Prize for literature; Legally adopts ***Arlette Elkaïm***

1968 Gives public support to student uprising in Paris, and condemns Soviet intervention in Czechoslovakia

1969 Mother dies

1970 Becomes editor of ***La Cause de Peuple***

1971-72 Three volumes of ***The Family Idiot*** published

1976 Feature length documentary ***Sartre by himself*** released; Becomes blind

1980 Publication of final interview with Benny Levy; Dies on 15th April

1949 France gives Vietnam sovereignty

1951 Centrist coalition formed in French elections, but falls a year later

1952 Anti-French rioting in Tangier

1954 French retreat in Indo-China; French troops sent to Algeria

1958 De Gaulle wins elections

1960 Rioting in Algiers

1962 Rioting in Paris against OAS, far-right group against Algerian independence

1968 Warsaw Pact troops enter Czechoslovakia; Student riots and workers protests in Paris

1970 Gauche prolétarienne banned by French government

1977 General strike in France against austerity programme

1978 Left wins absolute majority in French elections for first time

2. Influences on Sartre's Thinking

At the heart of Sartre's existentialism lies a detailed account of consciousness that draws upon the phenomenology of René Descartes (1596–1650), the empiricism of David Hume (1711–76) and the metaphysics of Immanuel Kant (1724–1804). This chapter will therefore begin with a brief introduction to these great thinkers' ground-breaking ideas in order to give context to the intellectual background of Sartre's philosophical education, before going on to look at how the work of Søren Kierkegaard (1813–55), Edmund Husserl and Martin Heidegger (1889–1976) influenced Sartre's thinking.

What Can We Know?

Sartre argues that his understanding of consciousness begins with René Descartes' discovery of the *cogito* or the 'I think'. This is what I fundamentally *am* – I am a thinking thing, a substance whose main attribute is thought. How do I know this? In the *Meditations on First Philosophy* (1641) Descartes asks you, the reader, to try and imagine that the world around you does not really exist and is simply a hallucination put into your mind by an evil demon. You have been deceived into thinking that you are reading a book, that you are surrounded by whatever objects are currently in the room, and that somewhere there is washing-up to do. You can doubt the existence of the world, including the existence of your body, but you cannot doubt that your mind exists – at least at the point at which you are thinking. After all, who would be being tricked? I think (*cogito*) therefore I am (*ergo sum*). At the heart of consciousness (of books, of washing-up) lies *self-consciousness*, an awareness of the existence of the self.

This central notion was questioned in Hume's *Treatise on Human Nature* (1739). He did not deny that consciousness existed. Of course, there is an awareness of reading the book in front of you that is currently taking place. However, Descartes' move from the *appearance* of the book in front of you to the existence of a thinking thing (a *res cogitans*) was a move Hume could not make. To say that a thinking thing exists, one must be able to access the thing that is thinking, not the thoughts themselves. Whenever we attempt to discover the mind as a substantial entity, producing thoughts and receiving sensations, all we discover is more thoughts, more sensations – more appearances! Hume (reluctantly) was willing to say that the nature of the self remained unknown, even if we know that experiences occur.

For Descartes, consciousness is the activity of a substantial self, whereas for Hume, there is no accessible self to speak of. Hume is unsure how a constant flow of perceptions can appear to be coherent if there is no 'self' behind the scenes to which those perceptions appear. But, in the absence of empirical evidence, he can only suspend judgement. Immanuel Kant's gigantic *Critique of Pure Reason* (1781) fuses together both Descartes' and Hume's theories to come up with a solution. What if, he says, there is no strictly Cartesian *res cogitans* (thinking entity)? What if, in principle, that which goes on below the surface of what appears before the mind is inaccessible? That this is because what is directly accessible to consciousness is structured by a framework of underlying principles that make coherent experiences (or *phenomena*) possible, rather than being a constant flux of colours, shapes and sounds?

Kant proposes this idea as a *transcendental ego* – an inaccessible 'I' that provides the structure for the phenomena we experience, including our own sense of self. The *cogito* is now divided over two levels, somewhat stripped of its traditional substantial basis, but not left empty. The appearance of the world is shaped by the *a priori* structures of the mind (independent of experience). Consciousness is shaped by what goes on *transcendentally* (beyond appearances). The world that exists outside of the mind – what Descartes would have considered to be made up of matter or physical substance – is unknowable. The *thing-in-itself* (what there is beyond appearance) remains hidden.

What is shared by each of these thinkers is the view that what appears before our minds – from our perceptions to our thoughts – is beyond dispute. The fact that there are *appearances* is transparent and indubitable. However, there is something we do not have direct access to that needs accounting for, that creates a sense of alarm when we do not get to access it and that will require increasingly elaborate philosophical gymnastics (beginning with Kant) if we are to give a full account of it. This can be the world of objects around us, or whatever lurks behind the scenes of our own experiences. Sartre would go on to form his own unique existentialist phenomenology through his engagement with other great minds.

Søren Kierkegaard: the Father of Existentialism

On 1 August 1835, a young man struggling with physical ill-health and constantly haunted by a sense of melancholy sat down to write in his journal. The entry could be seen as a personal statement of intent and an unwitting manifesto for not only himself but also for several generations of philosophers and artists to follow:

> *'What I really lack is to be clear in my mind what I am to do, not what I am to know, except in so far as a certain understanding must precede every action. The thing is to understand myself, to see what God really wishes me to do; the thing is to find a truth which is true for me, to find the idea for which I can live and die.'* (Kierkegaard, 1960)

Such words could be the opening lines of an introspective work of fiction or the voiceover during a slow tracking shot of an apartment at the start of a noir thriller. This is fitting, as most of the author's works were written using pseudonyms with little or no public acknowledgement from the man himself. Søren Kierkegaard may have aided the publication, but *someone else* wrote the notebooks that he discovered, and *someone else* edited them – or so the prologue would say. However, in the journals, we see the true Kierkegaard grappling with something much worse than an inner demon. He is having to deal with himself.

Kierkegaard was raised as a Lutheran Protestant and had grown dissatisfied with the cultural landscape of a newly democratized Denmark. Society was becoming little more than a collection of people that were dissolving into their social roles and becoming cookie-cutter versions of others. The ethical code of the day was simply to follow the rules and be a good social animal. This was not being helped by the ubiquity of the works of Georg Wilhelm Friedrich Hegel (1770–1831), whose idealism had taken hold of not only the universities but also the Church.

Fig. 8 Søren Kierkegaard.

Any simplification of Hegel's philosophy is automatically an over-simplification and giving it full exposition so that it can be understood would take up a greater volume than the original work itself. All that is necessary here is to grasp that, first, Hegel wrote some of the most impenetrably difficult works of philosophy ever written. Second, that his philosophy – pushing further than Kant's work – saw the world as a mental construct with an ultimately rational structure. Through the constant overcoming of the contradictions inherent in everything from the basic concepts we use to construct our reality (subject/object, finite/infinite) through to the way we organize our society, an end state will emerge in the form of absolute knowledge and a perfect political state.

In the same journal entry, Kierkegaard asks himself why Hegel's philosophy would do him any good. Whether it is a discussion of the political state or of the objective world, what good would it do to construct an account 'of a world in which I did not live, but only held up to the view of others'? Hegel's account of absolute knowing sees knowledge as something held in the mind but not lived. His whole philosophy begins with principles which he follows through to their own logical conclusions (note that Hegel had to invent an entirely new system of logic to accompany this). In his parody of Hegel's work, *Concluding Unscientific Postscript* (1846), Kierkegaard says that Hegel's philosophy is something 'to both laugh at and weep over'. He believed that Hegel should have left the work as a delightful thought experiment but, instead, he made the mistake of taking it seriously. What is worse, Kierkegaard says, is that philosophy has turned into a kind of exhibition where people display their theories for the scrutiny of others. If it is reviewed thoroughly and designated as correct, then the written work of the philosopher is held up as a sign of that thinker's greatness (regardless of how they live the rest of their lives).

It was not just the fact that Hegel's system was far too abstract that Kierkegaard found distasteful. Hegel felt that every contradiction within a concept or state of affairs (a political system or historical moment) leads to a resolution that melts the contradiction away – albeit for a new one to arise until the end point is reached. For Kierkegaard, no synthesis exists in such neat terms. Life may be full of contradictions and paradoxes, but the presence of those absurdities – from our reasoning to our quest for meaning – are at the very heart of our lived *subjectivity* in the world. It is part of what makes us a living being rather than a cog in a machine. For Kierkegaard, Hegel is just another figure that is hammering humans into an objective set of rules that govern behaviour. What bureaucracy is for the state, Hegelianism is for society and religion.

People must be shaken out of their objectivity and take charge of the choices at the heart of their lives – not once but over and over in a repetitive reaffirmation. Kierkegaard argues that people need the freedom to *become what they are*.

Kierkegaard's works treated philosophy as a form of provocation. He does not aim to deliver the truth to the audience in the way Hegel had hoped to. Kierkegaard removes himself from the picture and adopts the stance of a real (though fictitious) point of view that challenges the reader. Kierkegaard wanted to continue the work of Socrates (470–399 BCE), the gadfly of Athens. Socrates would engage in dialogues with those Athenians that boasted of their knowledge of goodness, truth and beauty (among other things), by playing the affable innocent abroad. He would question the interlocutor, asking for clarification and pointing out inconsistencies in their thinking, until they tied themselves in knots. Socrates' noble aim was not to make people look foolish but to get them to realize their own ignorance – the first step towards gaining true understanding. Kierkegaard did the same through his pseudonymous writings. Each text presents a case that the reader must engage with. The book does not give the truth but 'takes away' knowledge, forcing the individual to choose for themselves. Both Socrates and Kierkegaard use the term *maieutikos*, or midwifery, to describe their work. Socrates does not deliver wisdom like a postman delivers a letter. He delivers it by helping someone else give birth to it from within themselves, with them doing all the major work. Kierkegaard wishes for his readers to start acting as engaged individuals with their own thoughts as real *subjects* rather than passive objects.

Kierkegaard would be heralded as the father of existentialism, despite not using the term himself. Numerous concepts from within Kierkegaard's work appear throughout Sartre's writing: anxiety (angst) in *Being and Nothingness* and *Existentialism is a Humanism*; the absurd in his early novels; subjectivity and authenticity in his ethical and political writings, as well as his intricate descriptions of psychological states from a first-person perspective that litter all his fictional and phenomenological works. For both Sartre and Kierkegaard, we are living beings, not abstract entities existing in reason. We live real concrete lives, but we are largely drifting thoughtlessly until something jolts us into awareness of our situation. This terrifying moment is a point where we can return to the world in wilful ignorance or make a commitment about how to live. Kierkegaard wants us to realize that a single work by a philosopher tells us nothing of what a philosopher is thinking. This is shown through how they live, just as a single baptism or confirmation does not determine our status as a Christian. One ought to act knowing that eternity depends upon how the entire life is lived, not a single moment. Even as an atheist, these thoughts ripple through Sartre's writings. Take Sartre's *Existentialism is a Humanism*, where he elaborates on his concept of bad faith, a form of self-deception where we attempt to avoid being responsible for our actions (discussed later in Chapter 5). Kierkegaard chides the Christian who does not live as Christ does but deceives themselves and others by going to church each week, just as Sartre attacks those who claimed to be enemies of fascism but stood idly by as it swept across Europe.

What is most interesting about Kierkegaard's placing in Sartre's philosophy is that there is little-to-no sustained engagement with his work. Even Sartre's paper *Kierkegaard: The Singular Universal*, presented in 1964, only uses Kierkegaard to approach issues concerning biography and how Sartre's new method would deal with it (rather arrogantly, considering it was a UNESCO conference on Kierkegaard!). Nonetheless, Kierkegaard continues to crop up, if not by name, then obliquely in the language that Sartre adopts. In fact, at the end of his life, during a discussion with his personal secretary Benny Lévy on the subject of despair, Sartre says:

> *'Yes, I spoke of despair, but as I have often pointed out, I don't see it as the opposite of hope [...] I have never felt despair, nor have I ever, even remotely, seen despair as a quality I could possibly possess [...] Thus, it was, in effect, Kierkegaard who greatly influenced me on that. [...] His words seemed to be very real to others, and I wanted to account for them in my philosophy. It was in fashion.'* (Sartre quote in Cohen-Solal, 1991)

As we will see, Sartre sees despair as something that cannot be split into a simple binary of despair/hope, nor does he see it as something that automatically creates inaction and defeatism. While Sartre denies that he has felt despair (and in the interview with Levy says he dislikes Kierkegaard) his influence is noticeable.

Husserl's Phenomenology

Many of us have our own existential crises at some point (Who am I? Why am I here? Why was I born? What does it all mean?), but few of us go on to undertake a rigorous analysis of the nature of consciousness. Sartre explores how the gratuitous nature of

Fig. 9 Edmund Husserl, 1900.

being leads to anxiety and nausea in his fictional works. But, driven by a need to understand the nature of being itself, it is in his most famous philosophical work, *Being and Nothingness*, that he looks at the pure theory of the matter. Sartre's discovery of Edmund Husserl in the 1930s, followed by his reading of Heidegger during the 1940s, drastically overturned the way he had thought about the world and the self. Their philosophical approach is known as *phenomenology*, the theory that the structure of consciousness itself is to be investigated from a first-person perspective. Phenomenology (from the Greek *phainomenon*, relating to 'what appears' or 'what is shown') was originally conceived as a scientific way to describe what consciousness is and what it does. Think back to our discussion of Descartes previously. He had argued that our first-person experiences could be used to argue the existence of a substantial non-physical self. After a long detour through Kant's idealism, philosophy arrived at phenomenology – analyzing those same first-person experiences.

Phenomenology was first developed by Husserl. He was born in Prossnitz, Moravia, in the Austrian Empire (now Prostejov in the Czech Republic) but studied mathematics and philosophy in Berlin and later Vienna, where he attended lectures by psychologist Franz Clemens Von Brentano (1838–1917). Brentano argued that investigations of consciousness had hit a dead-end. Each attempt to understand the mind comes loaded with metaphysical presuppositions – whether Cartesian, Humean or Kantian – that stop a truly objective investigation of consciousness taking place. Empirical scientists were doing their best but were more concerned with biology than they were in understanding the conscious experiences that occur within a subject. What was required was a truly scientific *descriptive psychology* that gives a presumption-free account of the conscious experiences we have when performing various mental acts.

Husserl's own approach started somewhere close to Brentano's and ended back with something akin to Kant's, but it was always Husserl through-and-through. He never simply replicated or made minor adjustments to whichever philosopher he took influence from, but always rethought the whole idea from the ground up again. However, this does make a thumbnail sketch of his work difficult, as understanding his work with precision will require a detailed account of those that came before. He took Brentano's original project seriously and constantly battled with how a purely objective account of subjective experience could be given without any distortions caused by cultural, philosophical and personal biases. This was a back-to-basics exploration of Descartes' *cogito*, but without the trappings of notions of 'mental substance' or 'transcendental ego'.

Let us think as Husserl did: I am sitting in my garden with my laptop. In the background, I can hear running water. It is a pleasant sound and I enjoy hearing it. I stop to pay attention to it and realize that the sound of the water is making me thirsty. I think of a nice cold beer. I do not just hear running water either. I hear a fountain in my pond. I cannot see the fountain, but it is not the sound of a leaking pipe or an overflowing sink, otherwise my experience would shift to panic. The sound is expected or anticipated, as I switched the fountain on myself. If I took all of these experiences as they appeared to my consciousness and analyzed them in terms of the experience I have (the bubbling sound), the meaning attached to it (a fountain) and the way in which my consciousness orientates itself towards that content (expectation, attention, hope, worry) then I may start to understand not only how our conscious experiences work, but also be able to tap into the nature of what consciousness is. I would effectively be trying to explain how meaningful experiences of enjoyment of fountains and desire for a cold beer emerge from the constant flow of experiences that Hume discussed. During one period of his work, Husserl even thought this would shed us of the idea that objects are hidden behind our experiences and return us to 'the things in-themselves'.

To cope with this task, Husserl asks philosophers to set aside all the ideas and language that have been used to describe our experiences thus far (what he calls *bracketing*) and adopt an attitude of suspended judgement (or *epoché*), thus ridding ourselves of any presuppositions whatsoever, including any about the existence of the objects themselves. What we are left with is pure appearance (what he refers to as a *phenomenological reduction*) – a purely *descriptive* account of consciousness and its actions relaying what appears. Think about my experience of the garden mentioned above. On one level, focussing on my experience brings me to individual items like laptops and fountains, but this already involves a certain prejudice (e.g. I already know that *this* is a laptop, used for writing this book). I should do my best to leave all presupposition behind, stripping away the fact that I know what the objects are, thus leaving myself with a pure experience. This should then start to reveal the structures of consciousness itself. Husserl wants us to fully occupy a mental state, regardless of how mundane it is, and intuitively grasp its essence. This would not only help us to explain what it is to have a particular conscious state, but also what consciousness *is*. This was going to be a project much more extensive than just analyzing mental states to understand their component parts.

What Sartre recognized in Husserl's phenomenology was a development of thought that reflected his own thinking. In his *War Diaries* (1984), he writes:

> *'Husserl had gripped me. I saw everything through the perspectives of his philosophy [...] I was "Husserlian" and longed to remain so. At the same time, the effort I'd made to understand—in other words, to break my personal prejudices and grasp Husserl's ideas on the basis of his own principles rather than mine—had exhausted me philosophically for that particular year. [...] It took me four years to exhaust Husserl.'*

Introducing Intentionality

Perhaps Husserl's biggest contribution to the discussion of the mind, in terms of concepts that remain in philosophical discussion today, is his development of the notion of *intentionality*. Intentionality is the way in which our conscious awareness is directed towards objects of thought, and this directedness (more often phrased as 'aboutness') stands as a central feature of conscious states. As Husserl later said (and Sartre repeated constantly), consciousness is always consciousness of *something*. It is never empty or without an object. At its simplest, my perception of my garden is *about* my garden; my desire to have a beer outside in the sun is *about* having a beer outside in the sun. Intentionality (from the Latin *tendere*, to stretch out towards) takes on a new life in Sartre's philosophy. He not only takes it to be a key feature of consciousness, but also describes consciousness itself *as* this perpetually reaching grasp towards an object. In typically Sartrean style, descriptions of intentionality drip with an undead, lurching quality, ghoulishly searching for something to complete itself. Take something as simple as his repeated references to thirst throughout *Being and Nothingness*. In one sense, the thirst is *mine*. On the other, I am nothing more than the thirst itself. '[Thirst] knows itself as thirst at the same time as the drink satisfies it [...] Desire itself tends to perpetuate itself; man clings ferociously to his desires' (Sartre, 1943). Firstly, he writes as though thirst exists as a form of consciousness itself rather than just a thing that my consciousness is aware of ('thirst knows itself'). Secondly, it is a form of consciousness that is reaching out for something, propelling itself forwards towards the glass of water that will complete it. The drink that quenches the thirst is also the thing that makes the thirst realize itself. Of course, thirst always returns, returning from its annihilation again and again, and yet it is man that clings to these desires. Our sense of self seems parasitic upon thirst, tiredness, shame, indifference, joy, and so on. As we shall see in Chapter 3, Sartre's ability to write unnerving accounts of human psychology in his fiction added a poetic twist to the dry academia associated with phenomenology.

Heidegger: Fundamental Ontology

When Husserl retired from his position at the University of Freiberg in 1928, he gave his seat to his assistant, Martin Heidegger, who had recently published his mammoth work of phenomenology *Being and Time* (1927). Husserl had seen his own work as a continuation of Brentano, leading to a rigorous scientific philosophy called phenomenology which remained in the spirit of his teacher while radically questioning it. Heidegger did much the same with Husserl. From his perspective, Husserl had begun (quite openly) to revert to the exact baggage that phenomenology was trying to avoid. Husserl felt that our experiences did require a Kantian transcendental ego to give them coherence. Furthermore, he still spoke of 'consciousness' and 'essences' which were preloaded with philosophical presumptions of their own.

While Husserl's philosophical baggage-smuggling led Heidegger to conclude that his later works had not remained faithful to the phenomenology that he created, the young mentee was also concerned that his mentor's *epoché* and phenomenological reduction left out too much. No true reduction was possible because that is not how we are. Husserl was right to point out that I hear the water as a fountain, but the fountain itself is something connected to other things (water, ponds) which serve other purposes (making my garden pretty) and which are produced by other people (the person who dug the

Fig. 10 Martin Heidegger, 1960.

pond, the person that made the fountain), and so on. Our experiences are experiences of a *world* – an intelligible system of interconnected objects and meanings – that are already up-and-running when we discover them. To attempt any sort of complete reduction stripped of all presuppositions is not only impossible but also leaves out part of what it is to be us. We experience *Being-in-the-world*, always enmeshed in a world of activities or projects that we are undertaking, somewhat unreflectively.

This endlessly hyphenated use of the term *Being-* is central in the move from Sartre's interest in Husserl to Heidegger. Heidegger thought that the original philosophical questions, of which modern philosophy is simply an echo, were *ontological*, i.e. questions about Being. Being gets a capital-B because it relates to something more fundamental than its use in 'Are you being good?' or 'He is being arrested'. Any discussion of 'being' something already assumes that we know what 'being' means, just as using the word 'is' presumes a use of the word 'is' that denotes what it is to 'be' something in this context. Aristotle (384–322 BCE) made this his prime concern in attempting to categorize areas of existence (politics, biology, art, physics, ethics) and explain what it is *to be* in relation to those areas, in order to understand them better. Over time, this concept was gradually forgotten and philosophers simply turned the question of Being (What is it to be?) into a series of enquiries that treated Being as if it were being (an entity). Take Descartes as an example. To 'be' a human is simply to be made up of two types of things: a mind and a body. However, this does not explain what it is *to be* a human. That requires its own specific *fundamental ontology* with its own methodology and terminology.

For Heidegger, the discussion of ontology brings us to phenomenology. I cannot separate the objects that appear around me from the specific era that I live in, what Heidegger would call the *historicity* of my perspective. I find myself *thrown* into existence, then I simply blend into what the world is doing around me (what Heidegger calls being *fallen*). These are not states of being that I can shed off in order to uncover my true nature. This is what it is to *be* the kind of being that I am. The term Heidegger gives to the kind of beings we are is *Dasein* (being-there). This is not to be understood as a consciousness because a majority of what we do is not truly conscious. It is the routine unthinking behaviour of an individual in the world. This is no more noticeable than when we engage in our daily activities. I am currently writing this book with the sound of the fountain behind me. I am not actually aware of any specific objects as such, nor am I aware of myself writing (until, of course, I start to concentrate on the fact that I was previously unaware of the fact that I was writing – but you can see how the following points could be brought back into line with this realization). Both subject and object disappear in an engaged activity of writing. The same is true of people who are cooking or cleaning, hammering, or building, (or reflecting on how much we have been concentrating on writing) and so on. Even most of our conversation takes the form of a disengaged passing back-and-forth of whatever our culture considers to be typical chatter ('idle talk'). *Dasein* is *Being-in-the-world.* It is 'to be a mode of being' that is already in a world of things with purpose and function, lost within them.

For Sartre, Heidegger's influence came at an opportune moment when the war had a very real impact on his thinking (see Chapter 1). In February 1940, he described in his *War Diaries* how Heidegger's 'influence has in recent times sometimes struck me as providential, since it supervened to teach me authenticity and historicity just at the very moment when war was about to make these notions indispensable to me' (Sartre, 1984).

It is clear that Sartre's own philosophy borrowed from both Husserl and Heidegger. His own work is a continuation of Husserl's attempt to explain the fundamental *a priori* structures of consciousness, trying to find what consciousness is by exploring its contents. However, Heidegger's question of *Being* also lies at the centre of his approach and the idea of us as being-in-the-world is something Sartre wishes to take seriously. What we find is an attempt to investigate our lives as beings that are caught up in an existence, always actively engaged in our environment, while still trying to understand the mode of Being that consciousness is. As with Kierkegaard, it would be difficult to summarize every part of these great thinkers' work that directly or indirectly influenced Sartre. Descartes' *cogito* was the point of departure, but these were his fellow travellers on the journey.

3. Phenomenological Ontology

Anyone brave enough to tackle Sartre's magnum opus, *Being and Nothingness*, will know that it is an imposing text filled with a dictionary's worth of terminology, both invented and borrowed. But if we want to understand Sartre, then contact with this work is unavoidable. The discussions within this account reappear in one form or another across all his theoretical works, as well as in his plays and novels. In this chapter we will explore Sartre's *phenomenological ontology*, or his attempt to explain the nature of Being (or existence) through the methods used within phenomenology. For Sartre, the world contains two types of beings: those that are conscious and those that are not. Another way of putting it is that the world *appears* a certain way, so what appears, who it appears to, and what appearance *is* must all be accounted for within any fully developed ontology. Even appearance itself has its own way of being. This involves a series of moves back-and-forth between mundane examples and complex theory; between attempts to describe the structures of Being and descriptive accounts of appearances; and between revelation and our reactions to it.

Contingency: 'Being' Before *Being and Nothingness*

The typically existentialist account of Being (given a capital letter to distinguish it from everyday uses of the term) is first found in the novel *Nausea*. Written while Sartre was living in La Havre, the story follows the slow breakdown of a character as he unravels the superfluity of existence. The protagonist, Roquentin, realizes that behind the intelligibility that he imposes onto the world, there really is nothing but a bare existence. In one of the book's most famous scenes, Roquentin stares at a tree root in the park and thinks about what it is to exist. Regardless of whether he describes things in terms of their functions or categorizes them by type, nothing gets him to the core of *this* tree root. What is left is a 'frightening, obscene nakedness' (Sartre, 1938); an object that is purely contingent, superfluous, gratuitous, or in Sartre's terms, '*de trop*' ('too much'). The nausea that the novel speaks of is the realization of the contingency of things, not a feeling of sickness. It is a discomfort, a mode of being, in which the individual falls into a 'semantical nihilism' (Danto, 1985) and the intelligible world falls away and leaves behind an undifferentiated raw Being.

Contingency is to be understood in opposition to *necessity*, and Sartre had already been working on this concept philosophically for many years prior to *Nausea*. Necessity occurs whenever something must be the case. Think of necessity in terms of 'if x is true, then what *must* also be true?'. Imagine I say 'squares exist'. It logically follows that if 'squares exist' is true, then 'something with four sides exists' *must* be true, because it is an essential feature of squares that they have four sides. Now think of Being. If 'Being' is a fact – it just *is* – then nothing necessarily follows. Anything which follows – from squares existing, to our own lives occurring – is not by necessity but just happens to be the case. In fact, Being itself is not necessary. It could have been the case that nothing existed. Everything is superfluous and has no greater meaning in-itself.

While we could see this as all too dramatic to take seriously, the nausea described above is a useful introduction to Sartre's ontology. On the one hand, there is Being as a whole. It is a *plenitude* or fullness, as complete as it will ever be. The past is gone, the future is not yet here, and so Being exists in-itself as it is. However, what we experience is something more than that. The world is filled with histories and biographies, purposes and meanings, potentialities and possibilities. This is because reality is *intelligible* to a conscious being that *synthesises* the various elements to make a *world*. The world is this totality of things arranged in such a way as to be intelligible – so how does consciousness make something intelligible of something contingent and meaningless? What *Nausea* strips away is what *Being and Nothingness* attempts to explain.

Being-in-itself

The closest we can come to describing Being, according to Sartre, is that 'it *is*': it 'is *that*, and outside of that *nothing*' (Sartre, 1943). Sartre wants to explain that if Being is a fullness – a complete '*what is*' – then whatever else exists is simply a mode of that Being, or a way in which that Being is. What Sartre has called Being also gets referred to as *being-in-itself*, or the *in-itself*. It is that undifferentiated raw existence that 'is not created, changing, temporal, necessary, physical or spatial' (Cox, 2008). However, Sartre will sometimes use the phrase to describe non-conscious things around us. The laptop in front of me could be referred to as an in-itself, as it is a non-conscious mode of Being. It is an intelligible part of the overall unintelligible mass and so its mode of being is simply to *be*.

Why undifferentiated? Sartre does not mean this literally in the sense that everyone is one lump of matter. He is not saying that objects turn into primal sludge or a seething mass of energy when they are not being looked at. Outside of my window I can currently see three trees. I only know this because I counted them. Before that I thought of them in the collective, as 'trees'. Whether I see three trees, or individual trees, or a cluster with an indeterminate amount, all depends upon how my consciousness divides them. That does not mean that there is nothing there unless I think there is. It means that whether there are three trees, or a cluster, is a feature of how I frame that view, not the world itself. The world just *is*.

If intelligibility is imposed onto the undifferentiated world, how do I get an idea of this capital-B 'Being-in-itself'? Phenomenologically speaking, when I look at a book, I am consciously aware of the part I am currently seeing, but that appearance also contains within it an indefinite number of other aspects that I know the object has, even if I am unaware of exactly what those aspects are. I know that it contains multiple pages that I can flick through to reveal printed words. I know that the back cover will also contain information, and that I can read what the name of the book is on the spine. The simple set of colours, shapes and textures that come in through the senses do not tell the whole story of my perception of the book: it is experienced *as* a book, *as* a book I am about to read, and *as* a book that I hope is entertaining. Every object that I am conscious of overspills the phenomena I experience, but these other aspects (known and unknown) remain as possibilities of other phenomena. The fact that my experience of the book contains knowledge of this overspill is what Sartre calls the *infinite in finite*. It is the closest we come to understanding being-in-itself, and it is just one part of the structure of our conscious awareness of the world. While trying to grasp Being directly is impossible, we can understand that part of the way in which the world is structured for us is that something always escapes our perspective. Being is coextensive with appearance, but 'surpasses the knowledge we have of it and provides the basis for such knowledge' (Sartre, 1943) or what Sartre calls being *transphenomenal*. This is not a judgement that we make after the fact, but part of the very structure that makes the world intelligible as a collection of objects.

Before we move on, it is worth raising an important epistemological point here. Descartes' conception of the world separates physical objects off from consciousness. We have direct access to our mental states and how things occur within our sensations, but knowledge of the world is trickier. We know that the world *appears* to exist, but we must try to *prove* that it really does. Hume and Kant seem to follow this line of thinking even as they reject it. For Hume, whatever is hidden is unintelligible. For Kant, what is present can only be explained by what is hidden. For Sartre, however, nothing is hidden. Transphenomenality presents everything as it is. Nothing is kept from us. Being-in-itself stands before us as it is, even if our attempts at making it intelligible only allow it to be disclosed one aspect at a time.

Being-for-itself

The second important mode of Being is *being-for-itself*, or beings that are conscious. Sartre does not want to simply describe what it is like to be conscious (although existentialism is concerned with this). He also wants to explain how consciousness is structured: what is consciousness and what is it to *be* a consciousness?

It is here that discussions of Husserl and Heidegger reappear. First, Sartre agrees that consciousness is *intentional*, so it is always consciousness of something (as mentioned above). Second, he adds that the for-itself is *being-in-situation*. Its *situatedness* is its engagement with reality, mainly through the fact that it depends upon a physical body to exist, and the way in which it responds to this dependence. Third, the for-itself is already *being-in-the-world* (taken from Heidegger). The world is the intelligible arrangement of things within which I conduct my daily life, and this world presents itself to me as a series of objects that I want, expect, find, discover, pursue, and many more including their antonyms. Being in the world means to 'radically lose oneself in the world through the very revelation that causes there to be a world' (Sartre, 1943). The world comes into being because a consciousness starts to think of objects as more than just things. Each object relates to another, which relates to wider fields of activity. The book you are reading links to philosophy and Sartre, but also to publishing and writing – and therefore to work. Work relates to human need, human endeavour, and so on. The undifferentiated being-in-itself is made into a world of objects by a for-itself (a consciousness), which then falls into that world and loses itself within it, understanding itself only in relation to the activities it undertakes and the things it is surrounded by.

This may describe elements of what it is to be a conscious being, but what is consciousness itself? Descartes separates the mind from the body, and thus to be conscious depends upon having (or being) a soul – a *res cogitans* or thinking substance. What Sartre questions is precisely how this would work. Descartes is, after all, his point of departure and so he accepts that we have direct access to our own conscious experiences and thoughts, and that self-consciousness (awareness of oneself) is possible, in a sense. However, Descartes' account of the self only views it in terms of *reflective self-consciousness*, or introspection. Introspection is where we view our own mental states, turning our mental gaze inwards to reflect on our own mind. Like Hume, Sartre has issues with this, but his argument goes beyond the simple fact that we never see the self directly. Instead, it examines how consciousness itself is structured.

Think about how we watch a TV show. When I direct my eyes towards the screen, my mind separates off the television from other objects. Everything else becomes *ground* (or the undifferentiated background upon which things appear). This means that some objects are eliminated from consciousness, what Sartre calls *ignorance* (Sartre, 1989). Likewise, other objects have distances created between them. The people on the screen are separated off from each other as distinct objects. The world appears by us separating things out. This includes myself: if I did not separate myself off from the TV then I would be indistinguishable from it. Everything would be a single solid mass. Consciousness occurs not just by aiming itself at objects to create gaps between them, but by creating a gap between ourselves and the world. This happens simultaneously. Consciousness does not pre-exist the intentional objects, nor does it get brought into being by them.

To explain this, we should revisit Kant and draw a distinction between a *subject* and *consciousness*. Consciousness is awareness or experience of the world and – for us at least – of whatever is in our own minds. The subject is the thing that is having the experiences and performing the introspection. Kant changed the course of philosophy by suggesting that the subject (the 'me') is not only the observer of the experience but is also the *maker* of the experience. In other words, we put necessary structures on experience in order for it to make sense to us – we put it through a filtering or a moulding process. So experience is an action that structures and unifies.

In a similar way, for Sartre there is simply Being acting in such a way that consciousness emerges as an activity. Consciousness is something that Being *does*. If consciousness is always directed towards some object or other, and that object is something outside of it (of consciousness), this means that consciousness is always 'outside of itself' (Sartre, 1943). This is what Sartre refers to as *transcendence*. If I am consciously aware of the TV, then the TV exists as an object of consciousness, but as we all know from being engrossed in any activity, we lose our sense of self within that. I am not constantly thinking 'I-am-watching-TV-I-am-watching-TV' throughout, because I lose myself in the activity. My consciousness is outside of itself, aimed at the world, grasping at what it is *not*. However, Sartre agrees that all consciousness is a self-consciousness. To experience pleasure or thirst is to experience *my* pleasure or thirst. Descartes' account of this remained too reflective: he sees our ability to introspect and pay attention to our pleasure as enough to make his point. But Sartre disagrees. This simply moves the problem up a level because

I can always ask whether the experience of 'paying attention to pleasure' includes consciousness of 'myself paying attention to pleasure', and so on to infinity. To avoid this, Sartre argues that all consciousness includes a *non-reflective self-consciousness*. Part of the structure of consciousness includes the element of being 'mine', even when I am engrossed in a show and lose all reflective sense of self.

The question can be asked again: What *is* the for-itself? Let us think Sartre's account through thus far. First, consciousness comes into being as something that separates itself off from an object outside of itself. It aims at an object and says 'this', while positing itself as 'not-this'. Second, it never manages to see itself directly. Even in introspection, what we grasp is another appearance, another phantom of ourselves that is just in the corner of our view. However, there is always an in-built non-reflective self-consciousness that gives us a sense of self within each experience. Finally, we should bring in the fact that Being *is*. It is a fullness in-itself. This means that being-in-itself creates gaps within itself. In our case at least, a body (part of the in-itself) *transcends* itself and reaches out into the world, but only by creating a denial that it is that world.

This is Sartre's contribution to the discussion of consciousness we discussed at the beginning of Chapter 2. In his attempt to provide a very Kantian description of the structures of consciousness, he rejects Descartes' idea of a thinking substance and edges towards Hume's account that there is no self (or at least not one that is intelligible). What Sartre concludes is radical. Consciousness 'is not what it is and is what it is not' (Sartre, 1943) – but what does this paradox mean? Let's go back to me sat in the garden. The fountain is a self-contained object, being-in-itself, out there in the world. If I were merely a self-contained being then I would have no more consciousness than the fountain. In order to be conscious of the sound of the fountain, the being sat on the bench outside must transcend itself, i.e. it must perform an act of *being not what it is*. It also needs to make sure that it does not become identified with the fountain so that it can be conscious of it, so it experiences itself as *not-the-fountain*. Ultimately, consciousness is the *negation* of the Being-in-itself. It can only be understood as *not-being*. That is not to say it does not exist, but that it exists *as* a negation (a 'not') of Being itself, and so *it is what it is not*.

Disturbingly, this means that there is no substantial self. There is no transcendental ego behind the scenes making sense of everything, and no substance holding the *cogito* in place. In *The Transcendence of the Ego*, and later in *Being and Nothingness*, Sartre develops the idea that our notion of self is 'outside, *in the world* [...] like the ego of another' (Sartre, 1936, author's italics). Just as I explain the actions and thoughts of another person by positing the existence of a hidden mind, the same goes for myself when I reflect upon my own thoughts and actions. In *Being and Nothingness*, this leads to the development that we can never fully be what we are. We are always a gap within Being itself. Consciousness can only exist as this constant transcendence, a continual lurching outside of itself. This lack of foundation means that we endeavour to be an *in-itself-for-itself*, a being whose nature as a for-itself grounds it as if it were in-itself. With typical flair, Sartre writes that 'Man is a being whose project is to be God', and the fact that a final coexistence with ourselves will never occur leads to a conclusion straight out of his fiction: 'man is a useless passion' (Sartre, 1943).

Nothingness or Not-being

Sartre's explanation of the structure of Being makes him consider *nothingness* (or *not-being*), not as the alternative to Being or as an internal sense of absurdity and despair, but instead, it is understood phenomenologically and ontologically: 'no-thing-ness'. Things can *be* or *not-be*, with *not-being* as much a feature of things as *being* is. Take Sartre's famous example that echoes his childhood experience of his grandfather's party (see Chapter 1). I go to a café expecting to see my friend, Pierre. I scan the room for him, but all I do is *not see* him anywhere. I see faces that *are not* Pierre. The room *lacks* my friend.

Two forms of not-being appear in this example: first, when I take each person as *not-Pierre*; and second, when Pierre is *not-present*. In one sense, the café simply *is*. There is nothing in the room which is *Pierre's absence*. However, it is true to say that Pierre is absent in a way that a prehistoric caveman is not. A prehistoric caveman is not absent because no one expects him to be present, nor is his presence a possibility. However, I do expect to see Pierre, it is a possibility that I will see Pierre, and it is true that these people are not him.

Sartre claims that consciousness enables the for-itself to grasp non-being. The world not-being the way described is a possibility. Possibility itself involves non-being, in as much as there are things which are *not-yet*, just as imagination involves us mentally conjuring up what *is-not*. This is all possible because of transcendence, our ability to go outside of ourselves and our situation. We can think and act beyond what is present to us at any given time. What Sartre calls *negativities* involve an act of *negation* (denial) or *nihilation* (making into nothing). They are 'little pools of non-being' within the world (Sartre, 1943).

What Sartre is proposing is that non-being, or *nothingness*, is a central part of the structure of consciousness within the world. However, without consciousness there is no nothingness. 'Man is the being through whom nothingness comes into the world' (Sartre, 1943) because only through consciousness can things be designated as 'this' and 'not-this'. As consciousness itself is not an actual entity but a gap within the in-itself, 'Nothingness lies coiled at the heart of being – like a worm' (Sartre, 1943). Ontologically, the negations and nihilations that exist within the world are dependent upon there being a more fundamental negation: a non-being; a consciousness. That non-being is the for-itself.

Thinking About Sartre's Ontology

Let us sum up Sartre's overall ontology. Being ultimately has two different modes: being-in-itself (non-conscious things) and being-for-itself (consciousness). Without consciousness to direct its attention towards things, Being is an undifferentiated whole. It just *is*. Consciousness produces objects through its *intentionality*, its way of aiming at aspects of reality and separating them off from each other to make them into a meaningful world of things. Consciousness can do this because it can *transcend* its current state and *negate* whatever is in front of it. Furthermore, the only reason it can do this is because it is itself a negation that does not identify itself with any of the physical things around it.

Any discussion of ontology must begin somewhere. We can begin with the world and build ourselves into it, or perhaps we begin with ourselves and structure the world around us. What Sartre is attempting to do, in the wake of Husserl and Heidegger, is to try and envisage both at once, woven tightly together so that thinking of one must involve the thinking of the other. His early phenomenological works are a valiant attempt at this difficult task.

Reactions to Sartre's philosophy from within phenomenology were varied. Heidegger's response to Sartre's philosophy was that it was still trapped inside metaphysical thinking and he accused him of misunderstanding much of what appeared in *Being and Time*. Merleau-Ponty was less dismissive but developed a line of phenomenology that introduced detailed discussions of neuroscience and psychology. With psychology moving towards scientific experimentation and away from Freudian psychoanalysis, Merleau-Ponty's view of the subject was more in keeping with the times. He gave a much bigger role to the body in both phenomenology and ontology, which took readers away from the realms of Being and non-being.

Parallel to this, the world of analytic philosophy was finding Sartre's work to be objectionable. Analytic philosophy, represented in Sartre's time by the Vienna Circle (a group of philosophers and scientists who met regularly between 1924–36 at the University of Vienna) and the English philosopher Bertrand Russell, placed an emphasis on clarity of language, rigorous logical analysis, and empirical verification of ideas. Sartre's terminology can appear as a series of gestures containing partial truths that slowly build up a picture of something fuzzy, without providing anything that could undergo serious philosophical scrutiny. While Sartre can be said to reveal one possible truth – that subjectivity and consciousness are never grasped clearly and only gestures are possible – it also left many philosophers with the feeling that nothing substantial was being said. The Vienna Circle wanted clear logical arguments and claims that could be empirically verified. Sartre did not seem to be offering this.

With damning critiques coming from both within phenomenology and outside of it, we can see that Sartre's philosophy requires further explanation. Whatever universe we have – contingent or otherwise – it *does* enable consciousness to exist. The next big question is *how*? If all that exists is Being but somehow, within the midst of that, a gap or rupture appears that is consciousness, how does that happen?

Although Sartre does not explicitly endorse a materialist world view in *Being and Nothingness*, the American philosopher Hazel Barnes (1915–2008) notes that by *Critique of Dialectical Reason*, he had admitted that all evidence seems to indicate that living bodies and inanimate objects are all made of the same molecules (Barnes in Howells (ed), 1995). This means that whatever mechanism makes consciousness occur must be part of the physical universe. In theory, then, there must be a scientifically testable approach to finding this mechanism. The key issue is how one could test Sartre's account to see how being-in-itself negates itself to become a conscious being. How does one test for negation taking place within Being? How does one find a non-being? Or is all this metaphor and poetry? If it is poetry, that would not mean that the Vienna Circle could not appreciate it as such, but neither does it mean they would think it should be taken seriously as philosophy.

Defences of Sartre's work could avoid the issues above by getting us to return to Sartre's project from the beginning. First, Sartre's intention is not to provide a scientific account of anything but to create a phenomenological one. It is only ever going to extend to understanding consciousness and the way things appear to it, and perhaps his literary and poetic writing style is integral to that sort of approach. If we try to step beyond that and show what is underneath the surface and behind consciousness itself, we have not only misunderstood Sartre's project, but we are also assuming that we can give a full (scientific) account of consciousness from the outside. That isn't to say Sartre's account is complete, but perhaps studying brains or running experiments in labs just will not do.

Second, Sartre could argue that his account of the for-itself is structural. It is an attempt to show the way something would have to be so that it could be conscious of something else, and then work that through as thoroughly as possible. Sartre would say that as no one else can experience our consciousness, and as we have certainty about our inner experiences, phenomenology is the best way to uncover the workings of the conscious mind. However, this places too heavy an emphasis upon the analysis of consciousness itself without asking enough about where consciousness fits into the physical world. Merleau-Ponty had already started to investigate this in his own work by introducing neuroscience into his phenomenological analysis, suggesting that understanding consciousness required more than introspection. Several decades later, philosophers like Daniel Dennett (b.1942) would begin questioning the veracity of our first-person reports as a method of understanding the mind. The Cartesian claim that our accounts of the contents of our own experiences are incorrigible were being undermined by modern cognitive science. In *Consciousness Explained* (1993) Dennett suggests that we adopt what he calls *heterophenomenology*, or a phenomenology by others, not ourselves. According to him, each person's own reports should be taken seriously as reports of what things appear like to them, but this must be placed alongside the objective facts about the environment and the brain of that individual to get a full account of why that person had the experience that they did. Those phenomenological reports are accompanied by third-person observations by another individual that takes the subjective aspects as one part of something that can be explored systematically under controlled conditions.

Let's take a simple example, as used by Dennett in the work above. Imagine you see a longhaired woman without glasses dash past you, but when you report on what you saw later on, you say that you saw a shorthaired woman with glasses run past you. Now imagine that I reveal to you that your account is incorrect – the woman that ran past you did not match your description – but could you explain what your mind was doing during that experience? One option is that you originally saw the longhaired woman as she is, but your mind created a false memory that was able to remove any recollection that you saw a longhaired woman in the first place (what Dennett calls *Orwellian revision*, where the accurate original perception is overridden by a false memory). Another option is that the initial perception you had was false and thus the memory is an accurate reflection of what you originally perceived (what Dennett calls a *Stalinesque revision*). When such scenarios are recreated under controlled conditions, test subjects will sometimes say that their experience suffered from an Orwellian revision, some will say Stalinesque, and others will be unable to tell. The person is unable to give an indubitable, incorrigible account of what happened in those circumstances.

What does this have to do with Sartre? With reference to the everyday case above and various scientific tests recreating such scenarios, Dennett explains that our first-person experiences have no way of distinguishing between whether they are Orwellian or Stalinesque. What is needed is a controlled environmental (in this case, we need to control what the person is being shown and how) and further exploration of what the brain is doing. My report of whether it *appears* Orwellian or Stalinesque (or whether I can't tell) is hugely important, but nothing in my experience actually determines one over the other. Phenomenology does not provide us with accounts that are beyond correction. What we *think* we experienced may not be what we *actually* experienced when we refer back to it, and so something beyond first-person analysis is necessary.

Sartre is probably right that a series of third person observations cannot tell us anything about our own conscious experiences (unless there are some incredible advances in technology in the future), but that does not entail that our own conscious experiences contain the key to understanding themselves. Heterophenomenology is just one example of the kind of ways in which Sartre's phenomenology can be scrutinised. We can take Sartre's analysis of what it is like to experience the world and our own mental states as sincere, but that does not mean we can use that as our sole source of understanding the human mind.

4. Radical Freedom

In the days following the liberation of Paris during WWII, Sartre started to write an article for *Les Temps Modernes*. He wandered the streets and acted as a witness in much the same way as he had in La Havre when writing *Nausea*. His philosophical writing was moving from phenomenological ontology and towards ethical and political concerns, as were his novels and plays. For those who have encountered existentialism before, it is this line of thought that stands out as the most paradigmatically 'existentialist' within Sartre's oeuvre. Existentialists argue that humans are fundamentally and radically free, but always situated within a world that both obscures our freedom yet also acts as a necessary background for its existence. In a 1945 article in *The Atlantic* entitled 'Paris Alive', Sartre explains:

> *'Never were we freer than under the German occupation. We had lost all our rights, and first of all our right to speak. They insulted us to our faces every day – and we had to hold our tongues. They deported us en masse – as workers, as Jews, as political prisoners. Everywhere – upon the walls, in the press, on the screen – we found that filthy and insipid image of*

ourselves which the oppressor wished to present to us. And because of all this, we were free.' (Sartre, 1944)

It is this paradoxical sounding claim that we will unpack in this chapter. Sartre's interest in freedom varies from attempts to explain its phenomenological and ontological grounding, through to discussions of our political freedoms and obligations. All these ideas become tangled together. We shall therefore begin with an underlying issue at the core of Sartre's thinking and develop our understanding from there.

The Proto-existentialists

In the late 1930s, Sartre had developed a growing interest in the other proto-existentialist of the 1800s alongside Kierkegaard: Friedrich Nietzsche. Nietzsche provided the flipside of the Kierkegaardian coin. His concerns were similar: the homogenization of individuals within society; the loss of tradition in the name of the Enlightenment; the sense of confusion that follows; and the banality of modern life that results. However, he presented a deeply atheistic alternative. Nietzsche heralded the *death of God*, witnessing the erosion of all value-giving institutions within society, and predicting a descent into nihilism (an absence of all values). Those with the strength of character to invent their own values would do so. Everyone else would do what they always did – retreat in fear and look for someone to protect them.

The issues appearing across Kierkegaard and Nietzsche's works are less to do with our actual ability to choose to do one thing rather than another, and more of a diagnosis of the present social sickness and a course of action. The 19th century created a new choice for humanity, and one that would begin to define the individual and force them into a process of *subjectivity* or *self-creation*: Who are you going to *be* from now on? Both thinkers explore the difficulty of such a task and write stirring accounts of the psychological hardship that one experiences in the face of it. Sartre's philosophy echoes many of these themes but with a deeper ontological foundation. The need to decide upon our values and commit to them is not just a product of a particular period of European history, but something that has always existed as part of the human condition. Being-in-the-world clouds the contingent nature of what we see as the nature of things, and thus it does not come to our awareness too often. When it does, we must fully accept our freedom or hide from it.

Existence Precedes Essence

When Sartre defended existentialism against its critics in the lecture 'Existentialism is a Humanism' in 1945, he said that what unites the existentialists is their agreement that *existence* precedes *essence*. The core of our freedom lies in the fact that 'to begin with [we are] nothing...there is no human nature' (Sartre, 1946a). *Being and Nothingness* had developed the claim that there is no substantial self. As a conscious being, the for-itself understands what it is not – it is not an unconscious being (a being-in-itself). So if it is not a being-in-itself, then it must be a 'not-being' – a nothingness – possessing no-thing-ness. In this way, the for-itself is free; it is free to create its being. We will develop this more shortly, but Sartre developed a shorter argument for our freedom that stems from his atheism and is less tied into his phenomenology (thus making it easier to grasp).

Sartre gets us to imagine a paperknife. The object is designed with a clear purpose in mind and its attributes are selected so that a goal can be achieved. In my mind there is 'the sum of the formulae and the qualities which made its production and its definition possible' – or its *essence* (Sartre, 1946a). This blueprint precedes the actual *existence* of the paperknife itself. If there is a God, then humans will have a shared essence or 'human nature' regardless of where and when they exist, because we are all products of that original design. As there is no God, man does not have a nature or essence prior to existing: 'man first of all exists, encounters himself, surges up in the world – and defines himself afterwards' (Sartre, 1946a).

The history of philosophy is filled with attempts to find the defining feature that separates us from everything else. Our reason, creativity, sense of justice or feelings of compassion could all be contenders, but Sartre would stress that none of these things define us. Our capacity to reason does not mean that we cannot choose to live as irrationally as possible. We can feel compassion, but not be compelled to act upon it (or perhaps we are made to feel that it is a sign of weakness). The presence of any characteristic to a human consciousness does not determine how it is interpreted or acted upon. It is only in retrospect that we begin to define ourselves. We create ourselves through our choices.

Facticity

A typical response to Sartre's account of freedom is to highlight everything about ourselves that we have no control over. We are born into a particular socio-economic system, with a particular set of physical characteristics and dispositions, and a ready-made world that is already categorizing us before we have any idea of what is happening (hence Heidegger's description of being *thrown* captures our situation so well). These things impose themselves onto us as having always been there and thus restrict our freedom. The fact that someone is born poor and lacks opportunities as a result limits the scope of their choices and reduces the actual options available – after all, being poor is seldom a life choice. This backdrop of resistance upon which we enact our free choices is the *facticity* of our situation.

There is no facticity that can completely negate our freedom, however. We could argue that death negates our freedom but, if we are dead, we simply do not exist and therefore we do not exist as an unfree being. With the Nazi occupation of Paris in 1940, various topics of conversation became crimes. According to Sartre, the prohibition simply alerted people to their radical freedom. Think about your life now. There are lots of things that are prohibited by law that you would never dream of doing, but you know people are in prison for doing them. There are also things you do every day that are not prohibited, and so you barely even think about them. Reading this book is one example. Now imagine that you were banned from reading this book. The simple act of reading this short introduction to Sartre is now something that you must make a choice about. You have become like one of those people in prison. They knew there were laws against what they wanted to do, but they chose otherwise. Your freedom is in your ability to conform and stop reading the book, or to defy the law and continue to read it. Even then, you can choose to read it in secret, or publicly to rally support from likeminded individuals. The ubiquity of restrictions imposed by the Nazis is what made people free, in the sense that Kierkegaard spoke about earlier. Everyone was forced to accept their subjectivity and choose. The very presence of adversity only serves to illuminate the fact that we are free. We *are* freedom, it *is* our facticity: 'I am condemned to be free [...] we are not free to cease being free' (Sartre, 1943).

Another objection might be this: Sartre denies that there is human nature but then says that we are condemned to be free – so isn't it human nature to be free? If some philosophers say that rationality or compassion are human nature because they are an inherent part of what it is to be us, then it could be argued that freedom is the defining characteristic of human nature. This misses Sartre's point. For him, it is our lack of nature that makes us free. Freedom is the 'nihilation of facticity' (Sartre, 1943). Our desires and thoughts reveal a series of possible *projects* to us through a *surpassing* of what we currently are. The word *project*, as well as the French *projet*, has multiple meanings here: first, an undertaking or 'project'; second, to cast forwards; third, the prediction of a future event. Our choices are projects (undertakings) based upon projections (forecasts, predictions) towards which we project ourselves (throw ourselves into). For example, I am starting to feel tired and need to wake myself up. I alight upon the idea of making a coffee, so when I've finished writing this sentence I will go into the kitchen and put the kettle on.

Temporality and Freedom

Facticity may be a necessary correlate of our freedom, but it also clearly limits our possible actions. We cannot choose to fly or grow another foot in height overnight, so would it be reasonable to suggest that our personality or character are also limits to our actions? If someone knows that they are lazy, are they free to choose to not be lazy or is it so deeply ingrained that it is as unchangeable as being flightless?

The simplest answer is that we can always change. The person who knows that they are lazy can choose to fight against their laziness. Sartre describes a gambler who is trying to quit. In doing so, they must begin to change their behaviour and restructure their world. For example, certain routes are now taken out of regular use so that they do not wander past the betting shop. The gambler has negated that part of themselves that is 'the gambler', thus realizing that this is not who they fundamentally are. However, they also recognize gambling as one of the projects that they could undertake – gambling is a *possibility* for their future. For Sartre, freedom and transcendence enable possibility. Objects and things just *are*, the in-itself just *is*. They exist within the present moment. Using phrases like possibility and potential can be misleading, as it makes the object itself contain its future. The future is not contained within the present moment. Possibilities and potentials belong to the for-itself, as it transcends and projects by nihilating its facticity. The gambler chooses his actions regarding gambling, and thus chooses *himself*.

This relationship between past, present and future appears in Sartre's work under a discussion of *temporality*. Sartre first tackled this issue back in École Normale Superieure, when he wrote about Bergson; he then continued his exploration when reading Heidegger. Temporality, rather than being the sort of divisible time we find on clock faces, is the internal sense of time that permeates our phenomenal experiences. An oft-repeated example is that of a melody or chord sequence in music. When listening to a song, you receive each note separately, but the second note of the melody is experienced in conjunction with the first. The first note has vanished, but it remains within your perception of the second, with just the right time lapse to be able to hear the difference between them. The present note holds a series of expectations of the one that will follow, thus always projecting towards a future that will be resolved or take a strange turn and do something unexpected.

Your entire present is also part way through an act decided in the past (such as sitting down to read this book), and towards your future in a constant surpassing of your present. In Sartre's terms, you are not fixed in this current moment but are *in flight* towards a goal, with no attachment to the past other than being in the middle of an action chosen earlier. In the kind of time that we measure with clocks, the past has gone, and the future is not yet here. All that exists in the present is a for-itself in the form of nothingness (no-thing-ness), constantly outside of itself and aiming towards a goal.

Nor is the choice in the past able to truly determine what we do without the possibility of another course of action being possible. That even goes for those personality traits and values that we would consider unchangeable. The definition of ourselves that we construct is based upon an initial choice that tells us who we think we are in the world – what Sartre calls our *fundamental* or *original choice*. Whenever we react to something, such as someone upsetting us, we tend to think that there is a 'me' and a 'not-me' way of responding. We will often say 'I am not myself at the moment'. What we mean is that our behaviour does not match the image of ourselves that we have constructed by interpreting our past actions. To say 'I am a jovial person' or 'I have a quick temper' is to take a view of ourselves that has been constructed from interpretations of individual actions and to then internalize these traits as if they are a fundamental part of who we are. This interpretation must start somewhere; at some point a *fundamental choice* was made that shaped how we interpret our future experiences. 'When a man says, "I am not easy to please" he is entering into a free engagement with his ill-temper, and by the same token his words are a free interpretation of certain ambiguous details in his past.' (Sartre, 1943)

In choosing who we are, we also *choose the world*. We create the way in which the things around us appear and how they are built into our reality. This gives us a series of points of reference in our past that allow us to say 'I can't do that, I'm not that sort of person' or 'I can't help it – I'm just lazy'. In one of the more brutal sections of *Being and Nothingness*, Sartre argues that, in choosing ourselves and thus choosing our world, we also literally choose the war we have (or in his case, had):

> *'If I am mobilized in a war, this is my war; it is in my image and I deserve it. I deserve it first because I could always get out of it by suicide or by desertion [...] for lack of getting out of it, I have chosen it. This can be due to inertia, to cowardice in the face of public opinion, or because I prefer certain other values to the value of the*

refusal to join in the war [...] Any way you look at it, it is a matter of choice.' (Sartre, 1943)

The Other

Another side of facticity presents itself in the form of the *Other* – the for-itself that is not me. Each other individual is a for-itself that chooses itself and the world around it. Sartre claims that the phenomenology of the Other (how the Other appears to me) is already a part of my understanding of the world. When a person walks into a room, I see the room as if I were them, thinking about what they are looking at and why. When you catch a train, you will often scan the compartment for a spare seat. The seats are not just viewed as 'seats for me' but as 'seats for the Other who got on the train at the same time'. Your choice to prioritize comfort over politeness makes the train carriage appear as a much more tense place than those who are willing to stand. The presence of Others has changed the world.

The presence of the Other is described in terms of conflict for much of Sartre's early work. This is the man who wrote that 'Hell is other people' in his play *Huis Clos* (No Exit/In Camera) in 1944. Others are always other freedoms, other 'for-itselfs'. If we are to pursue our projects, then we must factor in the presence of people with predictable natures and specified functions, and so we *objectify* the Other. We think of them as things with deterministic qualities rather than free agents within the world. I rob them of their transcendence, subjectivity and freedom. However, I am also aware of the fact that I am an object for the Other. I am both aware of having my freedom taken from me by *the look* (the gaze that objectifies me when I am aware of being looked at) and how my facticity appears to the other. Do I appear as I wish to? Are there things about me that they will make part of my perceived essence that I would prefer them not to? We engage with the Other in a battle of wills, attempting to reduce them to an in-itself.

The phenomenological aspects of freedom thus become more apparent when we start to think about the Other. Shame is only possible because of the other. Sartre indulges his taste for psychodrama by describing a peeping Tom watching someone through a keyhole in a fit of jealousy. The mere thought of someone catching him is enough to shatter the world and turn it into a moment of shame. This is only possible because I can experience myself as an object for the other – as *being-for-others*.

Freedom and its Discontents

The Other is not always the chief catalyst in these psychological torments, but they can obviously heighten problems when we come face-to-face with our freedom. Think of everything we have discussed thus far. We are radically free and not only choose ourselves but also choose the world. This fact is obscured by daily life, but there are moments when our freedom is thrown in our faces. At such a point there is no easy answer, and we find ourselves in the kind of moment discussed by Kierkegaard and Nietzsche at the start of this chapter. To use a phrase from Heidegger, later borrowed by Sartre, we are *abandoned*. In our choices, we are alone.

Sartre illustrates this with a case from his own experiences as a teacher. A student of his came to see him for advice. His brother had been killed in the German offensive of 1940, and since then the student had wished to avenge his loss. He lived with his mother and collaborationist father. His mother was suffering the loss of a son and betrayal by her husband, and as much as the student wished to flee to England and join the Free French Forces, he knew this would be one loss too many. If he chose to stay at home then he could provide immediate help to his mother, but *only* his mother. If he chose to fight for a wider cause, then this would not only be leaving his mother behind, but also runs the risk of playing a vague and indeterminate role in the struggle. What if he ends up behind a desk somewhere? Sartre's answer is as predictable as it is annoying: you must choose (Sartre, 1946a)

The bigger point here is that the student presents us with the full phenomenology of freedom. He knows he must choose and feels the sense of abandonment that comes with it. He is in despair over the possibility that his choice will be the wrong one or will be misused by others. We can see here that he has turned to others for advice, pushing the decision onto someone else, and yet the choice to follow the advice or reject it is his alone. Even if he resorts to reading religious scriptures or philosophical treatises, he still chooses which ones to read and how to interpret them into action. How does one 'love thy neighbour'? By joining the Free French or looking after one's mother? The individual becomes overwhelmed by *anguish*. Building on ideas from Kierkegaard, especially *Fear and Trembling* (1843), Sartre explains that 'fear is of beings in the world whereas anguish is anguish before myself' (Sartre, 1943). The extent and inescapability of our freedom is terrifying. Kierkegaard's exploration of this through God's command to Abraham to sacrifice his son is one way of approaching it, but Sartre drags it into the everyday: 'man is in anguish' (Sartre, 1946a).

Sartre's Account of Freedom Revisited

For many, Sartre's account of freedom is easily dismissed because it ignores the determinism that we see within the universe. If we start with physics then we can explain how chemistry works, followed by biology and then psychology. We can then start to understand society, economics, politics and so on. If I knew everything there was to know about that student – from his experiences to his biology, and the kind of society he was raised in – then I could know what he would choose with the same precision as predicting a solar eclipse.

In Sartre's defence, this perhaps misses the phenomenological nature of his analysis. When we experience the world, we experience ourselves as free subjects. His account is trying to explain the phenomenology of the experience we have of ourselves as something transcending the deterministic universe. Even if we fully believe in determinism, we do not experience ourselves as a being caught up in the ebb and flow of physical forces, as if we were no different to driftwood on a wave. What Sartre is exposing (in a similar way to Kant) is how freedom appears within our experiences, and how those sorts of experiences reveal to us the possibility of changing our course of action. Other choices *were* possible, and other choices *are* possible because our consciousness is not restricted to the here-and-now, but always surpassing 'being' towards something else.

Further confusion regarding Sartre's attitude towards determinism may occur because of another shift in his writing.

As he became more overtly political, his discussion of freedom became less phenomenological (What is freedom? How does it appear to us?) and more ethical (How should I live upon realizing my freedom?). Individual acts become of greater relevance to him than looking at the general underlying nature of freedom itself. *Existentialism is a Humanism* is partly to blame here. The lecture was meant to bring existentialism to the public, and Sartre admitted later how it was simplified to the point of distortion. The book can leave readers with the view that every choice is as open as every other, which Sartre denies throughout *Being and Nothingness*.

Sartre's view of freedom also came under fire from Marxists who believed that the economic conditions of society determine the lives of the people who live within those societies. They believed that explanations of socio-economic structures are necessary in understanding individuals, not merely an afterthought once we have completed a phenomenological analysis. Sartre had refused to join the PCF, or any political party for that matter, because of his dedication to his individual freedom. When this sort of thinking appeared in his philosophy, it drew fire from those who saw social relations as a fundamental part of establishing human subjectivity. Geörgy Lukács (1885–1971) clearly presented an ultimatum in the title of his book: *Existentialism or Marxism* (1948). He thought that to be an existentialist is to be an idealist who believes that the world reflects the mind, not the other way around. He believed that Sartre's thinking ignores concrete social phenomena and material conditions in favour of abstract theorizing, thus rendering any meaningful social change impossible. The Frankfurt School's Herbert

Marcuse (1898–1979) claimed that Sartre's theory of freedom remains an abstract mystification, ignoring the concrete socio-historical unfreedom that real beings live within.

Sartre was not unaware of these points. He had begun to address them in *Existentialism is a Humanism*, where much of the lecture is in response to Marxists who accuse him of bourgeois complacency and the reinforcement of an individualistic ideology. In 1969, Sartre gave an interview published as *Itinerary of a Thought* (in Sartre, 1948), in which he admits that *Being and Nothingness* fails to grasp the severe limitations placed upon individuals:

> *'For I believe that a man can always make something out of what is made of him. This is the limit I would today accord to freedom: the small movement which makes of a totally conditioned social being, someone who does not render back completely what his conditioning had given to him [The individual] interiorizes the relations of production, the family of his childhood, the historical past, the contemporary institutions, and he then re-exteriorizes these acts and options which necessarily refer us back to them. None of this existed in [*Being and Nothingness*].'* (Sartre, 1974)

It is with these criticisms and his own acceptance of them that we will begin the next chapter.

5. Responsibility

It is tempting to move from a description of Sartre's ontology to an account of what we could call an existentialist ethics. Sartre's attempts at an account of ethics remained either unpublished until after his death or were spoken of regretfully. Sartre himself disowned *Existentialism is a Humanism* as oversimplified and underdeveloped, which many scholars would agree with. It seems unfair to use an introductory guide to present ideas he never published, or that he disowned, as if they constituted a complete system. Some writers attempt to construct Sartre's ethics from what appears in his published work and what came to light after his death. This is a noble and enlightening project, and you are encouraged to explore this further. Instead, this chapter will give a selective overview of the development of his thought under the banner of his account of responsibility, as this not only allows us to explore some Sartrean concepts but also to see how his own attempts at responsibility shaped his work.

Bad Faith and Authenticity

In *Being and Nothingness*, Sartre explored a peculiar feature of our ordinary everydayness – a constant state of self-deception and denial that he calls *bad faith*. His analysis is without moral judgement; instead it presents a basic feature of how we relate to ourselves in terms of both our facticity and our freedom. Take a waiter in a café: 'the waiter in the café cannot be immediately a café waiter in the sense that this inkwell *is* an inkwell, or the glass is a glass' (Sartre, 1943). The inkwell is *in-itself*, an unconscious being without any transcendence or surpassing. The waiter is a waiter in that he is performing the role of being a waiter in a café. He knows the rules of being a waiter and so applies himself to that role. Of course, the waiter knows that his job is not his inner essence, but he is a waiter to the extent that he is hired as one (rather than being hired as an ambassador) and so acts like one. All of this is evident in his behaviour, which is always a little exaggerated and 'seems to us a game' (Sartre, 1943).

Sartre then indicates that the reason for the waiter's behaviour is to be found in demands made by society, so that he must perform a 'dance' suited to his role so that he becomes nothing but a waiter. 'A grocer who dreams is offensive to the buyer, because such a grocer is not wholly a grocer' (Sartre, 1943). So why the demands? If we go back to our discussion of anguish and all that came with it, we can see that the world is a lot easier to cope with if the Other has a clearly determined essence that renders them predictable. The waiter must pretend to be what he is not (a waiter) in a way that suitably convinces us that it is really a part of his essence so that he can keep his job. I deny both the waiter's freedom and facticity.

This denial of freedom and facticity does not end with others – we also do it to ourselves. A person is in a continual vacillation between states of self-deception, so that the idea of an essential self can be maintained, and we can be protected from anguish.

We package our past actions together to create an idea of an essence, which we use to guide our future choices. However, this gives us the opportunity to blame our present behaviour on that essence ('I can't help it – it's just who I am!'). We will then switch to accepting that we are not restricted to any fundamental nature by dismissing past actions as 'not who we are'. If who we are was deterministic, nothing could ever be out of character. We are a confused mixture of denying our facticity to emphasize our freedom, denying our freedom to emphasize our facticity, and sometimes both at once. For being-for-itself, bad faith is unavoidable.

Being and Nothingness explores the structure of bad faith and what makes it possible rather than presenting an ethical position. However, the ethical connotations of bad faith do appear in *Existentialism is a Humanism* and elsewhere. Bad faith is the attitude of the Quietists. Quietism has its own meaning in contemporary analytic philosophy, but Sartre is using it to describe those who said 'let others do what I cannot' and refused to fight for social change (Sartre, 1946a). His use of the term is borrowed from a derogatory name for a 16th century Christian movement that prioritised silent meditation and stillness above overt worship and vocal praise for God. In Sartre's view, if there was no certainty in the success of the resistance against the Nazis, then silent despair was the Quietists' chosen option. It is also in this text that terms like *cowards* and *scum* are elevated to technical terminology. Bad faith is a cover for the *cowards* that hid in fear and made excuses for themselves when they were 'only following orders'. It was in the ideology of the *scum* who saw themselves as a historical necessity, crushing other free individuals in the name of their own destiny. It was found in the *salauds* ('bastards' or 'swine', a term Sartre had used since his student days to describe the bourgeois class he was surrounded by) who lived in the *spirit of seriousness* – the view that reduced man to an object among others and treated ethics like a series of immutable laws of physics. Sartre proclaimed that if we accept responsibility for our choices, for our role in the creation of the world around us through that choice, and endeavour to act with honesty towards our freedom and facticity, then we would be acting *authentically*.

What Sartre's philosophy permits is a *radical conversion* – a moment where, upon realizing our freedom and the contingency of our fundamental project, we commit ourselves not just to recreating ourselves, but also the world. These basic notions – bad faith, authenticity, radical conversion – may not always have been used explicitly in Sartre's later writings, but they remain thematically in his work. Individuals living alongside others must take responsibility for what they and the world are and can be. This not only takes a dedicated self-creation but also engaged social struggle.

The Analyst of Society, History and the Individual

Alongside the philosophy, fiction, plays, screenplays and journalism, Sartre also wrote biographies. The most famous of these are *Saint Genet* (1952), about the author and thief Jean Genet, and *The Family Idiot*, a biography of Gustave Flaubert published throughout the 1970s in several volumes. The Genet manuscript had almost been thrown on the fire by the man himself after reading it. According to Sartre, Genet complained that the work had reduced him to an immutable statue without the freedom to act naturally. What Sartre was experimenting with was his own *existential psychoanalysis*, an attempt to understand the individual as they are while retaining existentialist ideas of freedom.

Sartre remained critical of psychoanalysis throughout his career but always saw something positive in it. Freud had developed a system which analyses the current personality, actions, and neuroses of individuals by exploring their past, especially their childhood. Sartre accepted that our past clearly has an influence on our present understanding of the world and self, but disliked the determinism in Freud's work, as well as the constant reference to the unconscious. In later works, he agreed that Marxism was guilty of overlooking individuals in favour of broad discussions of social class and economic structures but felt that modern psychoanalysis was little more than a loose collection of methods and an underlying mythology. He believed that a proper psychoanalysis (an existentialist one) was therefore necessary.

This psychoanalysis involves tracing back our choices to the self that we have constructed, then back to the fundamental choice that began that whole process. As mentioned before, this can lead to radical conversion or authenticity (something that was developed in therapeutic practice by R.D. Laing (1927–89)). What Sartre was increasingly willing to allow was the *internalization* of the social world around us, which is then *externalized* in our worldview and forms of behaviour. The fundamental choice that determines our sense of ourselves is changeable, but it appears within an environment that has already decided what we are and places such a heavy burden on us that acceptance of our life's project is almost inevitable.

What Sartre attempts to do with both his later psychoanalytic biographies and in his Marxism (which we will discuss shortly) is to use a *regressive-progressive method*, which he developed in his essay 'Questions de méthode' ('Search for a Method', 1957). We begin with what we know about an individual and give the fullest account that we can, before *regressing* to the historical background upon which the individual appeared. We then build a picture of what it is to be that person within those parameters (for example, to be a male, middle child in a bourgeois family in 19th century Denmark). One then *progresses* back to the individual, bringing the analysis of the situated individual with them, to produce a circular *totalizing* movement, by which the individual and their social surroundings are bound inseparably. What is not lost in this process is the individual – the lived subjectivity at the heart of this movement. They are neither an idea we have created, nor a dead objective fact. This is a fusing of existential psychoanalysis and Marxism that seeks to disclose the historical situation of our subject without losing the *subjectivity* of the individual, so that it engages us as analysts and readers.

Action by Disclosure

Being politically engaged does not always mean being on the frontline with a rifle in your hand. *Secondary action* is possible, that is, an indirect engagement which is nonetheless an important part of the struggle. For Sartre, writing is a secondary action that he calls *action by disclosure*. His phenomenology refers to consciousness as providing a disclosure of the world, where one part of reality (the solidity of a glass) is revealed to another part of reality (a human being). Writing can disclose the world to a reader, presenting it via the perspective of the writer. *What is Literature?* (1948) is a collection of essays and articles on the nature and purpose of writing with the aim of allowing us to understand the challenges faced by the writer in post-war Europe. Once we understand that language is a way of presenting the world, and that speaking and writing are actions we can perform, the author takes on a whole new responsibility. In choosing ourselves, we choose the world. In writing, we potentially shape the world for the reader. 'Man lives in the midst of images. Literature offers him a critical image of himself.' (Sartre, 1974)

Sartre sets about differentiating prose writing from other forms of art, including poetry. The painter wishes to produce objects, not signs or significations of objects. When they paint a picture of a house, they are creating a house as an object, but in the form of a painting. The painting can also be infused with anguish or grief in the way that it is painted, through the choice of colour palette, and so on. Poetry is in the same field as painting. 'Poets are men who refuse to *utilize* language' (Sartre, 1948, author's italics); for Sartre, they see words as objects among others within the world. Humans are *situated* within language and use words as instruments, whereas the poet allows themself to detach a word from its function. Poetic language exists in its own realm, detached from the reality that it usually signifies. We are expected to enjoy the words in the way one enjoys tonality, form or melody in other forms of art. This is not just a way of writing but an entire *attitude* towards language.

If poetry is an attitude, then so is prose. Sartre describes how language is felt and used as much as our body is, something we act through spontaneously and without thought, except where precision is needed. Losing our words renders us unable to act, to indicate, to understand, to persuade, to relate, to guide. Language is a tool to be used, and it is a tool used to disclose. The prose writer adopts this as their attitude and, by doing so, the reader can see the world but also see their own behaviour reflected in the writing. After seeing themselves reflected in the gaze of the Other in the form of writing, the reader cannot return to the world without considering their place within it. 'The function of the writer is to act in such a way that nobody can be ignorant of the world, and nobody may say that he is innocent of what it's all about' (Sartre, 1948). Only prose can do this, poetry cannot. Sartre even quips that he does not dislike poetry for this, in fact, the reason LTM hardly publishes any poetry is precisely because of how much they like it.

The project of the writer is displayed in the blank page before him, and the reader finds it in the book in their hands. For Sartre, reading is a synthesis of perceiving and creating. The writer delivers the object – including the project, the aim or goal of the writing – and the attentive reader must draw the meaning out. The *message* of the work is what the writer wishes to disclose and what is revealed through the active participation of the reader. Reading is *directed creation*, with the author acting as a guide through the work to reach the object, while allowing the reader to come to the discovery through unifying the various strands of the work. 'The writer appeals to the reader's freedom to collaborate in the production of the work' (Sartre, 1948). There is a joint enterprise, a 'pact of generosity'. 'The work of art is a value because it is an appeal.' (Sartre, 1948)

During his time as a student (and for the rest of his life) Sartre frequented the cafés of Paris' Left Bank and rubbed shoulders with important cultural figures of the day. *What is Literature?* contains his derisory account of the surrealists, Salvador Dali (1904–89) being one such example. According to Sartre, they spoke of destroying bourgeois values and creating chaos, including lots of references to 'exploding' and 'violence', but largely they produced controversial works of art that did nothing to change society, nor did they have any positive project about what would happen should the system collapse. During the same period in the USA, a group of black writers and poets jumpstarted what became known as the Harlem Renaissance – a movement that sought to rethink what it meant to be black in America. By the 1930s, a similar movement had emerged amongst African intellectuals, writers and politicians from French-speaking colonies that had moved to Paris. The movement was called *Négritude*. Just as the Harlem Renaissance wanted black Americans to rediscover themselves outside of white stereotypes, so *Négritude* wanted Africans to discover what it meant to be black outside of colonialism. Literature became a vital part of activism.

Early signs of Sartre's own attempts at holding a mirror up to his own social group appeared in *Anti-Semite and Jew* (1946): his attempt at addressing the treatment of Jews prior to and during WWII. A clumsy and naïve work in many respects (so much so that it made George Orwell refer to Sartre as 'that windbag'), it nonetheless has moments of brilliance. In summary, Sartre says, 'If the Jew did not exist, the anti-Semite would invent him' (1946b). Sartre digs down into the mindset of the anti-Semite to uncover where their passion for hating Jews comes from. He finds nothing in Jewish people themselves to explain this, but only in what the anti-Semite has used the figure of the Jew to stand in for. Through fear of his own freedom and responsibility, the anti-Semite creates the image of the Jew to allow them to explain their own failings and justify their violence against others. The first chapter of the text is a witty but penetrating account of not just how anti-Semitism functions as a form of bad faith, but also how many social prejudices emerge out of a desire to dissolve oneself into a crowd to avoid alienation.

The naivety appears in his account of Judaism itself, directed through his understanding of Jews as an ethnic group in Europe, rather than members of a religion with a long and diverse history. For Sartre, even the Jew comes to understand their Jewishness through seeing themselves as Other. This reasoning is not itself at fault, especially as Jewish philosopher Hannah Arendt (1906–1975) develops this theory in *The Origins of Totalitarianism* (1951), but Sartre is seemingly unaware of the rich history of the Jewish people, and thus his account misses the mark. What Sartre does manage to capture is the complicity of the French people: their willingness to dismiss Nazi sentiments as 'just opinion' rather than actively opposing them; the latent anti-Semitism in the liberal's suspicion of anyone who puts their cultural identity above an abstract notion of humanity; those who remained silent because they were not anti-Semites nor Jews. Sartre felt great guilt for his own complacency, and his account of the liberal even reflects comments he had made himself in the past. As awkward as it can be, Sartre was making an early attempt at understanding how our view of ourselves and the Other is shaped by our choices *and* our surroundings.

What started awkwardly in *Anti-Semite and Jew* matured into the writings collected in *Colonialism and Neo-Colonialism* (1964). Every page acts as a mirror through which the reader sees themselves and their own complicity. The Algerians must be free so that they can create their own identities and their own world. French society is nothing more than the actions of the French people. Sartre concludes that if French authorities are using torture in Algeria, then it is bad faith to adopt the position of the passive observer.

The committed writer commits to being the mediator and guide. They recognize themselves as both a person in the world but also as *a writer*. The reader is *historical* – they appear within a particular culture with its own mythologies and interpretations of history, its own class structures and so on. The reader is placed within that world and views it from their perspective. The writer engages with that historical agent, but the writer is also historical. Society views the writer in a particular way, and the writer must then decide who they are to be. They decide how they write, who they write for and what they write about. To be committed to writing is not just to be committed to producing words on paper as part of a job, but to choose to write *as a writer* – as one that engages the freedom of the other. In his fictional works, Sartre writes so that the world is presented to us in a way that engages our freedom so that we may collaborate in the creation of the work alongside him. We can then return to the world with a different view of ourselves and others, and thus act differently. From his existential psychoanalysis through to his passive–regressive method, the co-dependence of part and whole, society and individual must be thought through and communicated together to disclose how the world is. After that, it is up to the reader.

The Intellectual in Society

Sartre was a great writer and a great thinker. In a lecture series published as *A Plea for Intellectuals* (1965) and the interview *A Friend of the People* (1970) (both in Sartre, 1974), Sartre discusses the role of the intellectual within society. The intellectual may be a writer but need not use that as their medium. Likewise, a writer need not be an intellectual. So, what are intellectuals and what are their purpose within society?

Sartre began his philosophical career as a teacher, or as Sartre refers to them, a *technician of knowledge*. These technicians work within a specific field, whether they be teachers or doctors, scientists or engineers, and work with knowledge that is deemed *universal*; they work with fixed truths that apply everywhere and can be communicated to others through training. They are often drawn from the middle classes, or from those within the underprivileged majority who rise to a higher social class. Today we might call them experts or professionals, identified by their job more than anything else. As such, Sartre says, they fit in with the ruling ideology. They are trained within an education system to fit in with the demands of the ruling classes (in this case, a capitalist class motivated by profit) and so their ends *are not their own*.

The intellectual is 'someone who attends to what concerns him' and who those in authority see as someone 'who interferes in what does not concern him' (Sartre, 1974). He is – in the eyes of the powers that be – a *meddler* that oversteps their technical knowledge and starts to make judgements in other areas. Take someone like David Attenborough (b. 1926). He is a world-class naturalist, but not a member of parliament. Nonetheless, he frequently draws our attention to ecological issues and tries to mobilize us both in our private lives and in our political concerns. This is a very public example, but one does not have to be famous to be an intellectual – every technician of knowledge has this potential. We might take the idea of calling David Attenborough a 'meddler' to be quite the insult – but it depends upon who is saying it. While he is beloved by many, Attenborough does not just alert the public to facts about wildlife, but to an ethical struggle against the destruction of our world. He incites people to make demands and cause headaches for the government. 'Meddling' here should be taken with a pinch of irony. After all, Sartre knew that anyone in charge of one of the schools he worked at would probably have seen him as a meddler too.

Borrowing heavily from Marxist theory, Sartre unpacks the contradictory position of the intellectual and their own alienation within their social class. They have humanistic sensibilities yet recognize themselves as benefiting from social advantages that the majority lack. They cannot eliminate this inequality without eliminating themselves, thus they must throw themselves into projects that bring their advantages to the majority. They recognize that their current position is one dictated by the dominant social order. Their new project is one of radical action with the aim of creating a universal culture that avoids all the previous ideological trappings. Sartre is clear on this – rejecting the norms of the past is more than rejecting the current social order. It also involves a rejection of any mythology that sounds progressive but is not.

Here he is thinking of the way in which the proletariat have been glorified and fetishized within Marxism. The whole idea of what it is to be a member of a social class must be rethought for the present, not simply applied from abstract principles thought up centuries ago.

If we are to bind the extensive Marxist and Hegelian discussion across *A Plea for Intellectuals* to Sartre's writings of the 1940s, we can do so by considering what Sartre saw as the stages of the development of the intellectual. The intellectual is:

> '*suspect to the working class, a traitor to the dominant class, a fugitive from his own class who can yet never wholly escape it [...] Everywhere the intellectual is unassimilable [...] a defective product of the middle classes, compelled by his imperfections to live on the fringe of the under-privileged classes without ever becoming part of them.*' (Sartre, 1974)

The intellectual only avoids this through bad faith: they can become what Sartre's friend Nizan called a 'watchdog', or what Sartre calls a *false intellectual*, using ones position to reinforce the dominant ideology of the day. They can deny their roots in the middle classes by having too much humility and becoming an ineffective activist; or they could become suspicious and resentful of the under-privileged class that they are desperate to join. All of this is self-deception and denial in one form or another. The only authentic option is to grasp the whole situation in all of its contradictions. The intellectual must attempt to understand themselves within the society in which they find themselves situated and use what technical prowess they have in order to work alongside those who do not have the same advantages as part of a committed and ultimately radical project.

Sartre's ideas on responsibility began as a rebellion against the futility of the world in the form of a quite narcissistic dedication to one's own freedom. What it turned into was a 25-year-long exploration of the role of the individual in the creation of the world around them. He never found a simple solution, and no such solution was ever promised. Nonetheless, we do find recurring themes that remind us that we all play a role in the creation of our surroundings, even by refusing to engage with them. We do not all have to become writers or resistance fighters, but in Sartre's use of the terms, we can all be committed, and all be intellectuals in some form.

Conclusion

We began this book by considering whether individuals can be defined. There is no fundamental and necessary essence that determines any one being. By the end of the last chapter, we had explored the difficulty of trying to understand individuals in total isolation and outside of any historical context whatsoever. Sartre remains an important figure because he – along with the likes of Camus and Beauvoir – stand as the embodiment of a particular spirit and attitude that existed in post-war France, and which resonated with other parts of the world. 'Don't forget,' Sartre told an interviewer in 1959, 'that a man carries a whole epoch within him, just as a wave carries the whole of the sea' (Sartre, 1974). Accounts of the man himself are like a window into the past, revealing a single perspective upon a complex whole.

When Sartre died in 1980, Existentialism had been out of fashion for a quarter of a century, Marxism was going to disappear until a resurgence following the financial crisis of 2008, and phenomenology had been overtaken by postmodernism, post-structuralism and deconstructionism. Interest in Sartre's work appears to be mostly historical, with no real attempt to continue his existentialism occurring for decades. It is probably fair to say that Sartre was what was needed for a generation finding its path after the chaos of the early 1940s. Someone needed to steer the way between despair on one side, and blind faith on the other. Sartre reminded the public of the need for action and the dangers of both resignation to the status quo and the handing over of one's own dignity to dogmatism.

The remaining question is whether Sartre's work is of more than just historical interest to us today. There is no point in surmising what Sartre would think of the world today because, as he would point out, he does not live within this era. It would be to think of Sartre as an abstract being that could be dropped into a particular epoch like the application of a mathematical formula. Trying to work out what Sartre would say about our current social and political predicament also misses a deeper point: no matter what Sartre would say, it does not dictate what I must do. When we see the global environmental movement Extinction Rebellion occupying the streets of London in the UK, we are put into a position where we must choose whether to join them or let them do what we are not willing to do. Sartre's advice can be followed as instruction or dismissed as the ranting of an old existentialist has-been. That is up to each of us to decide.

The key to Sartre's work – as with any late philosopher – is to use him as a lens through which we view our present to uncover unseen dimensions in the situation. This can be in the field of academia: for example, two books used in the research for this text – *The New Sartre* (2002) by N. Farrell and *Using Sartre* (1994) by G. McCulloch – try to reinvigorate present debates in postmodern and analytic philosophy respectively by showing how Sartre's ideas open new conceptualizations of consciousness and freedom that can be enlightening, even if they are not wholly successful on their own terms. But the malleability of Sartre's philosophy is somewhat overlooked. The failings of his own project may have consigned him to the history books, and yet works like *Being and Nothingness* are startlingly innovative in their approach to traditional philosophical questions.

'[If] a writer pleases me [...] it's usually because he disconcerts me somewhat initially' (Sartre, 1974). This is how we should read Sartre. The experience *should* be uncomfortable because he is revealing things to us about ourselves. Sartre's work transcends the era in which he lived because there was a universality in what he spoke about. The condition of the worker in 1940s France or the colonized Algerian is incomprehensible to the modern reader in some respects, and yet we are presented with an image of ourselves through them. We are responsible for the world we currently live in, just as all of France was responsible for the torture of Algerians 'including the men and women who never stopped protesting against it. We are inextricably involved' (Sartre, 1948). The way to read Sartre here – hyperbole aside – is to see it as a provocation to analyse our role in the society in which we live. We may not literally torture others ourselves, and we may even protest when we hear about it, but Sartre was warning us against virtue signalling way before it was a common accusation against activists. Even those who speak out may do so in bad faith, and so no one should consider themselves beyond reproach or freed from guilt because they were vocal in their political beliefs.

Sartre does not present any easy answers, or the self-creation found on a *live-laugh-love* fridge-magnet, telling us that good things become manifest through positive thought. It would not be too hard to cherry pick a sample of quotes and mislead people into thinking Sartre believes we can do whatever we want to do, be whoever we want to be, and that the only people who fail are those who stop trying. He is not encouraging such narcissistic projects as 'living my best life'. On one hand, our lives do not gain meaning by posting a meme on social media. When he said that the genius of Proust is to be found in his works, he meant that no one is *anything* until they are actively pursuing it. On the other hand, we cannot expect that our hard work will always lead to positive outcomes. Even the most just causes can end in failure. There is no necessity to history. Goodness does not always emerge victorious in the end. For Sartre, these myths are ultimately counter-productive, even if they allow us to sleep more easily.

In a world that still contains a far-right and far-left division, sweatshop labour, genocide, questions of identity, and impending ecological disaster, Sartre's message of responsibility and freedom have never been more worthy of reconsideration. Sartre cannot tell us what we should do about these situations, but his writings stand as a reminder of the fact that we make choices – as difficult and constrained as they are – that either slot in with the way the world is and allow it to continue, or that set out to make a change. We cannot guarantee success, but there can at least be a more honest way to fail.

Bibliography

Works by Sartre

Sartre, J. (1936) *Transcendence of the Ego*. London: Routledge. (This edition, 2004)

Sartre, J. (1938) *Nausea*. Translated by R. Baldick. London: Penguin. (This edition, 2000)

Sartre, J. (1943) *Being and Nothingness*. Translated by H. Barnes. London: Routledge. (This edition, 2001)

Sartre, J. (1944) 'Paris Alive: The Republic of Silence', *The Atlantic* (1932–1971), Dec 1944, Vol. 174, No. 6, p43. Reproduced in *Paris Alive: Jean-Paul Sartre on World War II* (2021) by N. Gordon. Available at: https://www.theatlantic.com/international/archive/2014/09/paris-alive-jean-paul-sartre-on-world-war-ii/379555/ [Accessed 19 August 2021].

Sartre, J. (1946a) *Existentialism is a Humanism*. Translated by P. Mairet. York: Methuen. (This edition, 2020)

Sartre, J. (1946b) *Anti-semite and Jew*. Translated by G.J. Becker. New York, NY: Schocken Books. (This edition, 1995)

Sartre, J. (1948) *What is Literature?* Translated by R. Frechtman. London: Routledge. (This edition, 2008)

Sartre, J. (1960) 'Tribute to Albert Camus' in *Camus: A Collection of Critical Essays*. Edited by G. Brée. 1962. New Jersey, Prentice Hall.

Sartre, J. (1964) *Colonialism and Neocolonialism*. Translated by A. Haddour, S.

Brewer and T. McWilliams. London: Routledge. (This edition, 2006)

Sartre, J. (1967) *Words.* Translated by I. Celphane. London, Penguin Books.

Sartre, J. (1968) *Search for a Method.* Translated by H. Barnes. New York. Random House.

Sartre, J. (1974) *Between Existentialism and Marxism.* Translated by J. Matthews. London: Verso. (This edition, 2008)

Sartre, J. (1983). *Witness to my life: the letters of Jean-Paul Sartre to Simone de Beauvoir, 1926–1939.* Edited by S. de Beauvoir. New York: Scribner's; Toronto. (This edition, 1992)

Sartre, J. (1984) *War Diaries: Notebooks from a Phoney War 1939–40.* London: Verso. (This edition: 1999)

Sartre, J. (1989) *Truth and Existence.* Translated by A. Hoven. Chicago [Ill.]: University of Chicago Press. (This edition, 1995)

Sartre, J. (1993). *Quiet moments in a war: the letters of Jean-Paul Sartre to Simone de Beauvoir, 1940–1963.* Edited by S. de Beauvoir. London: Hamish Hamilton. (This edition, 1994)

Sartre, J. (1995) *Anti-semite and Jew.* Translated by G.J. Becker. New York, NY: Schocken Books.

Other works cited

Aronson, R. (2005) *Camus & Sartre.* Chicago: University of Chicago Press.

Bair, D. (1990) *Simone de Beauvoir: A Biography.* New York: Touchstone.

Barnes, H.E. (1974) *Sartre.* London: Quartet Books.

Barnes, H.E. (2006) 'Sartre's ontology: The revealing and making of Being' in C. Howells, ed. (1995) *The Cambridge Companion to Sartre.* Cambridge University Press.

Beauvoir, S. de. (1962) *The Prime of Life.* London: Penguin.

Beauvoir, S. de. (1981) *Adieux: Farewell to Sartre; followed by Conversations* *with Jean-Paul Sartre*. Harmondsworth: Penguin. (This edition, 1985)

Beauvoir, S. de. (1990) *Wartime Diary*. University Of Illinois Press. (This edition, 2021).

Beauvoir, S. de. (2006) *Diary of a Philosophy Student: 1928–29*. University Of Illinois Press. (This edition, 2021)

Bernasconi, R. (2006) *How to Read Sartre*. London: Granta.

Beyer, Christian, 'Edmund Husserl', *The Stanford Encyclopedia of Philosophy* (Winter 2020 Edition), Edward N. Zalta (ed.). Available at: https://plato.stanford.edu/archives/win2020/entries/husserl/. [Accessed Dec 2021]

Blackham, H.J. (1959) *Six Existentialist Thinkers*. New York: Harper and Row.

Charlesworth, M. (1976) *The Existentialists and Jean-Paul Sartre*. University of Queensland Press.

Cohen-Solal, A. (1991) *Sartre: A life*. Minerva.

Courtwright, D.T. (2001) *Forces of Habit: Drugs and the Making of the Modern World*. Harvard University Press.

Cox, G. (2008) *The Sartre Dictionary*. Continuum.

Cox, G. (2019) *Existentialism and Excess: The Life and Times of Jean-Paul Sartre*. Bloomsbury Academic.

Crowell, Steven, 'Existentialism', *The Stanford Encyclopedia of Philosophy* (Summer 2020 Edition), Edward N. Zalta (ed.). Available at: https://plato.stanford.edu/archives/sum2020/entries/existentialism/ [Accessed Oct 2021]

Danto, A. (1991) *Sartre*. London: Fontana Pr.

Dennett, D. (1993) *Consciousness Explained*. London: Penguin Books.

Descartes, R., Haldane, E., Ross, G. and Chavez-Arvizo, E. (1997) *Key Philosophical Writings*. Hertfordshire: Wordsworth Editions Limited.

Flynn, Thomas, 'Jean-Paul Sartre', *The Stanford Encyclopedia of Philosophy* (Fall 2013 Edition), Edward N. Zalta (ed.). Available at: https://plato.stanford.edu/archives/fall2013/entries/sartre/. [Accessed August 2022]

Farrell, N. (2002) *The New Sartre*. Bloomsbury Academic.

Gardner, S. (2009) *Sartre's 'Being and Nothingness'*. Continuum.

Goldthorpe, R. (1992) 'Understanding the committed writer' in Howells, C. ed., (1995). *The Cambridge Companion to Sartre*. Cambridge University Press.

Hayman, R. (1986) *Writing against: A Biography of Sartre*. London: Weidenfeld & Nicolson.

Kern, E. (1965) *Sartre: A Collection of Critical Essays*. Englewood Cliffs, N.J.: Prentice-Hall.

Kierkegaard, S. (1960). *The Journals of Kierkegaard 1834–1854*. London: Fontana Books.

Laing, R. and Cooper, D. (1964) *Reason & Violence*. London: Tavistock Publications.

McCulloch, G. (1994) *Using Sartre*. London: Routledge.

McDonald, William, 'Søren Kierkegaard', *The Stanford Encyclopedia of Philosophy* (Winter 2017 Edition), Edward N. Zalta (ed.). Available at: https://plato.stanford.edu/archives/win2017/entries/kierkegaard/. [Accessed Oct 2021]

Moran, D. (2000) *Introduction to Phenomenology*. Routledge.

Philip, T. (1964) *Jean-Paul Sartre*. London: Hamish Hamilton.

Rowley, H. (2007) *Tête-a-Tête*. Random House.

Rybalka, M. (1982) 'Sartre: A Short Chronology'. *The French Review*. Special Issue, Vol. 57, No 7, pp.131–133.

Seymour-Jones, C. (2008) *A Dangerous Liaison*. New York: Overlook Press.

Simont, J. (1992) 'Sartrean Ethics' in C. Howells, ed., (1995). *The Cambridge Companion to Sartre*. Cambridge University Press.

Todd, O. (1998) *Albert Camus: A Life*. London: Vintage.

Wheeler, Michael, 'Martin Heidegger', *The Stanford Encyclopedia of Philosophy* (Fall 2020 Edition), Edward N. Zalta (ed.). Available at: https://plato.

stanford.edu/archives/fall2020/entries/heidegger/. [Accessed August 2021]

Woodruff Smith, David, 'Phenomenology', *The Stanford Encyclopedia of Philosophy* (Summer 2018 Edition), Edward N. Zalta (ed.). Available at: https://plato.stanford.edu/archives/sum2018/entries/phenomenology/ [Accessed July 2021]

Biography

Benjamin Jones has been a lecturer in A-level philosophy since 2005, both professionally and whenever the chance arises, in a desire to help bring philosophy to the public. He completed his degree at the University of Birmingham, and his MA through the Open University while working as a lecturer. He spent most of his adult life so far trying to produce music, releasing albums and singles under the name Mitch & Murray through Regular Beat Recording Co. He lives in the Black Country, West Midlands, UK, and probably always will. This is his first book.

Acknowledgements

Thank you to all at Bowden & Brazil for this opportunity, especially Alice Bowden for her help, guidance and patience. Thanks to Dr Jonathan Birch for his invaluable advice. Thank you to Sarah Collisson for reading numerous rewrites of chapters and listening to my stream of consciousness. Thank you to family (immediate and blended) that gave support, especially my brother David who made me read *Nausea* and suggested I take philosophy at degree level, and my parents. Thanks to Dr Lauren Traczykowski and Dr Sarah White for generally pestering me to try and get something published. A special thanks to my daughter Alice, the infinity in my finitude, the necessity in my contingency.

Picture Credits:

Opening image: Jean-Paul Sartre, 1965. Unknown author (https://commons.wikimedia.org/wiki/File:Jean_Paul_Sartre_1965.jpg), „Jean Paul Sartre 1965", https://creativecommons.org/licenses/by-sa/3.0/nl/deed.en. Fig 1. Jean-Paul Sartre, c.1910. Unknown author (https://commons.wikimedia.org/wiki/File:Jean_Paul_Sartre_circa_1910.jpg), „Jean Paul Sartre circa 1910", marked as public domain, more details on Wikimedia Commons: https://commons.wikimedia.org/wiki/Template:PD-old. Fig. 2 École Normale Supérieure, Paris, c.1900. Héliotype : E. Le Deley, Paris. (https://commons.wikimedia.org/wiki/File:École_normale_supérieure,_rue_d'Ulm,_Paris,_vers_1900.jpg), https://creativecommons.org/licenses/by-sa/4.0/legalcode. Fig. 3 Simone de Beauvoir, date unknown. NiaVasileva (https://commons.wikimedia.org/wiki/File:Simone_de_Beauvoir_photo.jpg), „Simone de Beauvoir photo", https://creativecommons.org/publicdomain/zero/1.0/legalcode. Fig. 4 Simone de Beauvoir and Jean-Paul Sartre in Beijing, China, 1955. (Liu Dong'ao) (https://commons.wikimedia.org/wiki/File:Simone_de_Beauvoir_&_Jean-Paul_Sartre_in_Beijing_1955.jpg), „Simone de Beauvoir & Jean-Paul Sartre in Beijing 1955", marked as public domain, more details on Wikimedia Commons: https://commons.wikimedia.org/wiki/Template:PD-China. Fig. 5 Paul Nizan, 1924. Unknown authorUnknown author (https://commons.wikimedia.org/wiki/File:Paul_Nizan_1924.jpg), „Paul Nizan 1924", https://creativecommons.org/publicdomain/zero/1.0/legalcode. Fig. 6 Maurice Merleau-Ponty, date unknown. http://www.philosophical-investigations.org/Users/PerigGouanvic (https://commons.wikimedia.org/wiki/File:Maurice_Merleau-Ponty.jpg), „Maurice Merleau-Ponty", https://creativecommons.org/licenses/by/3.0/legalcode. Fig. 7 Albert Camus, 1945. Studio Harcourt (https://commons.wikimedia.org/wiki/File:Camus_Harcourt_1945.jpg), „Camus Harcourt 1945", marked as public domain, more details on Wikimedia Commons: https://commons.wikimedia.org/wiki/Template:PD-France. Fig. 8 Søren Kierkegaard. The Royal Library, Denmark, No restrictions, via Wikimedia Commons. Fig. 9 Edmund Husserl, 1900. Unknown author (https://commons.wikimedia.org/wiki/File:Edmund_Husserl_1900.jpg), „Edmund Husserl 1900", marked as public domain, more details on Wikimedia Commons: https://commons.wikimedia.org/wiki/Template:PD-1923. Fig. 10 Martin Heidegger, 1960. Willy Pragher creator QS:P170,Q2571685 (https://commons.wikimedia.org/wiki/File:Heidegger_2_(1960).jpg), „Heidegger 2 (1960)", https://creativecommons.org/licenses/by-sa/3.0/legalcode

Who the hell is
Aristotle
Amanda Forshaw
Accessible | Informative | Engaging

Who the hell is
Plato
Dr Karen Parham
Accessible | Informative | Engaging

Who the hell is
Michel Foucault
Dr Julian Molina
Accessible | Informative | Engaging

Who the hell is
Friedrich Nietzsche
Oliver Dixon
Accessible | Informative | Engaging

Who the hell is
Immanuel Kant
Dr Mark Robson
Accessible | Informative | Engaging

Who the hell is
David Hume
Dr Mark Robson
Accessible | Informative | Engaging

Who the hell is
Ludwig Wittgenstein
Dr Howard Peacock
Accessible | Informative | Engaging

Who the hell is
B. F. Skinner
Tom Buxton-Cope
Accessible | Informative | Engaging

Who the hell is
Jean Piaget
Dr Jessica Koehler
Accessible | Informative | Engaging

Who the hell is
Melanie Klein
Lucy Etherington
Accessible | Informative | Engaging

Who the hell is
Stanley Milgram
Kimberley Croft
Accessible | Informative | Engaging

Who the hell is
Karl Marx
Manus McGrogan
Accessible | Informative | Engaging

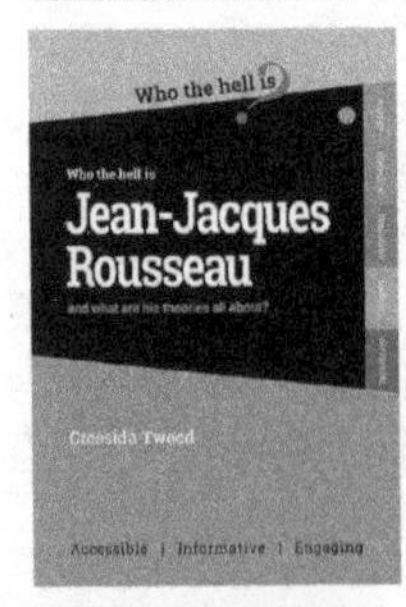
Who the hell is
Jean-Jacques Rousseau
Cressida Tweed
Accessible | Informative | Engaging

Who the hell is
Olympe de Gouges
Mina Moriarty
Accessible | Informative | Engaging

Who the hell is
Betty Friedan
Betty Londergan
Accessible | Informative | Engaging

Who the hell is
Erwin Panofsky
Alice Bowden
Accessible | Informative | Engaging

Who the hell is
Jane Jacobs
Deborah Talbot
Accessible | Informative | Engaging